# IT TAKES GUTS TO LEAVE THE RUTS

## HOW TO BREAK FREE FROM YOUR PAST, BE TRANSFORMED BY FAITH, AND REALLY LIVE!

ANNETTE DIXON

IT TAKES GUTS TO LEAVE THE RUTS



The resources in this book are provided for informational purposes only and should not be used to replace the specialized training and professional judgment of a health care or mental health care professional.

Neither the author nor the publisher can be held responsible for the use of the information provided within this book. Please always consult a trained professional before making any decision regarding treatment of yourself or others.

ISBN: 978-0-473-50225-6 (paperback)
ISBN: 978-0-473-50226-3 (ebook)

# Dedication

THIS BOOK IS dedicated to my amazing husband, my forever love, who has been a major part of loving me to wholeness. You were the first one to really love me (aside from God). You have always treated me like the most valuable person on earth. I am unbelievably grateful to God for you. Your unwavering, unconditional and steadfast love has been a huge strength and stability in my life, always cheering me on in whatever I put my heart to and to reach my highest potential in God. Your unswerving loyalty and constant belief have drawn out the best in me and made me who I am today.

To my four incredible, faith-filled daughters, who are my absolute delight and treasures. I am so grateful for your love and encouragement to write this book. I look at you and am thankful for the priceless privilege of being your Mum. I can never imagine not loving you with all my heart and cheering you on to reach your highest potential. Although you will always have your own challenges in breaking boundaries to achieve your goals, I am so indebted to God for saving me so that the generational curse was broken over your lives, and so you and my darling grandchildren would never have to endure or fight your way out of the same messed up childhood I did. You are the most wonderful mothers. Continue being the brave, strong women you are, making a beautiful difference in your spheres of influence and precious lives for eternity.

To my Personal Encourager, my Personal Counsellor and Guide, precious Holy Spirit, I owe everything to you. Without you, I wouldn't even be here. I am forever indebted to You. You are an expert at making something out of nothing. May Your love and hope shine through this book to save and restore many other precious, valuable lives.

# CONTENTS

# INTRODUCTION

All I can say is, who I am today is a completely transformed person compared to who I used to be; I have been transformed by faith.

I was the kind of person who had no self-esteem, courage, backbone, or opinion on anything. There is no way I could be writing, speaking, leading and encouraging people throughout the nation, or even feel like I had anything worthwhile to contribute, without the transforming grace of God.

My testimony is one of fear to faith. From debilitating, paralysing, soul-destroying, excruciating fear and anxiety that tried to hold me bound for years, to a life of wholeness, faith and courageous adventure.

I am a Jesus-lover, who continues to plumb the depths of His love and has found such treasures in His Word and unbelievable healing that is almost too unspeakably good to describe. I am also a seasoned pastor of 30 years, who has coached and counselled thousands of people on how to have a mindset makeover to line up with the word of God.

No matter to what extent the damage done, or the timespan, the Word of God is truth, and IT WORKS, yesterday today and forever! God's promises are true.

Perhaps you are thinking, 'Well, that might work for others, but it won't work for me." I used to think the same way, but when I threw myself on God's promises and dared to believe them for myself, depending on them for dear life, I found that they are truth. The Holy

Spirit is the best Counsellor in the world, and armed with some practical keys, you can work WITH HIM to see yourself set completely free.

Sharing my testimony and personal experience has been an encouragement to many people who had previously resigned themselves to staying where they were for the rest of their lives. As I have spoken on these topics over the years - privately, at churches, conferences, locally and internationally - I have had so many ask me to write a book. As a pastor, it is not always easy to share deep, personal areas of my life in public, and even more challenging to publish them in a book, but I believe there are people everywhere that the Holy Spirit wants to help and minister to in a special way.

Because of the practical tools I have learned as I've walked my own journey, I have been able to help many others out of dark places, and I want to make these truths readily available, to give others the hope and the steps out of these places.

This book will give you the tools to break through by realizing just how those old mindsets have kept you trapped and showing you how to change the way you think on a daily basis. It also has stories and encouragement from people who have turned their lives around by getting rid of their excuses or disadvantages and renewing their minds to line up with the Word of God.

At the end of the book, I have summarised key principles I have found are vital for our own mindset makeover and to teach and train our children, called 'Faith Bites'. There is such an epidemic of anxiety and depression amongst our littlest people in today's world, and it truly breaks my heart; they are like drifting ships without an anchor. If you can teach your children these life-altering principles on how to deal with their thought life and raise them with a positive outlook on life (as I did my own girls), it will build their self-worth, their resilience, their bounce-back ability and give them the tools they require to not only survive in life but to thrive.

## There is Hope

We all go through things in our lives that have a large bearing on what we are like. People hurt us, circumstances knock us around, and some of us have very tough things to work through, even though we put on a brave front on the outside. Some of us have deep hurts, and until we release them to God, they will only hold us bound. Many of us SAY we're set free in Christ, but our lives deny it. Only Jesus can get right down inside and deal with those things that keep us locked up in certain areas.

I believe Jesus wants us to risk being fully set free, in every area of our lives; free to be the person He has created us to be. Who wants to be held bound all their lives, when God wants to see that powerhouse of potential that's in you (that HE has placed in you) unlocked and released for His glory?

I didn't want my book to be just about depression. I didn't want it to be just about sexual or childhood abuse. I didn't want it to be about debilitating fear. As huge and life-altering as all those things are, the principles in this book will change ANY life situation. Because truly, if you really boil it all down, it's about the transforming power of faith.

We need to have a 'Mindset Makeover' to line up with the Word of God. No matter where you are at, or what you have been through, you too can leave those ruts. But I will warn you, it will take **guts to leave those ruts**!! Faith is definitely not a passive thing, but a fight to shift those old mindsets and automatic default responses. The biggest change comes when you summon the courage to rise and fight your way out with His help.

More than anything, I want to provide hope – that there is a way out. I am living proof! There IS life on the other side of that dark tunnel. You don't have to stay stuck like this for the rest of your life. There is HOPE and, if you give the Holy Spirit the chance, He will heal you completely. Better than new! The Holy Spirit is our Teacher, our Comforter, our Helper, the real Counsellor and the best Counsellor in the whole world – the only One!

## The power of testimony

"Tell your story. Not for fame or praise.
But to ease the pain of others."
(Yvette Mystakas)

When I was in my darkest place, I would have given anything for someone to take me by the hand and give me even a skerrick of hope to hang onto… a tiny lifeline to help me from being sucked down that plug-hole into a deep dark place; someone who would walk me through the practical steps to help me out of the hell-hole I was in. The reality is that unless you have been there yourself, you can struggle to fully understand how this cycle of darkness feels. And that's the power of testimony.

I have ministered in environments where people were in tears because they related so much to what I was sharing about my upbringing. They felt safe to be able to open up for the first time. They have joined our church because they knew they had a pastor who understood them and would be safe. I have also spoken in environments where people have looked incredulously at me as if I was from another world. Their world was so far removed, with almost no comprehension that these sorts of things even happen to people. It was almost like they wanted to remain removed, indifferent and dismissive.

The reality is that many times when I was in that dark place, I would try to say something, try to open up to a friend or family member, and I felt like they would make a glib or off-hand comment or not be interested, and that would just shut me down. It felt like they really didn't get it at all, and how could they? Sometimes our journeys are so complex to even put into words for ourselves, let alone for others, and so we end up shutting down even more and struggling on by ourselves.

When people hear someone who has been there and has the sense that they "get" them, it's such a relief! "Oh my gosh, they understand me. They can put into words exactly what I am going through." There's an instant connection, a sense that someone has been in this place before me, and a rising up of Hope. Testimony gives us the hope that not only has someone else has been there too, but they have overcome and moved forward in their journey.

## Nothing's impossible when we work in partnership with God

I've been teaching these Faith Principles to people for years - people who subscribe to my emails, have attended the churches we have led or groups we have taught, those who have had private counselling or coaching sessions, have attended conferences, meetings or classes or have been referred by friends.

Thousands of people (both male and female, younger and older) have put these techniques into practice and have seen God rebuild their lives to health, vitality and strength, IF they were prepared to put the faith work in. The revelation comes when we realize Faith is not a passive thing waiting for God to do it, but a fight, where we have to work in partnership with Him for the victory. One of the first things I learnt at Bible College was that Theology is all about "God's Sovereignty + Man's Responsibility". It's not all up to God. We have to work with Him.

Can I encourage you to read this book with an open heart, and a willingness to go to the difficult places? If you find something bothering you as you read, something is stirred up in your life, as the Holy Spirit begins touching on an area in your life, allow Him to take it and minister healing and release, gently, like only He knows how. Place it in His big capable hands. Don't fight it coming up! Lots of prayer has gone in for you, for those who will read this book. The Holy Spirit has arranged for this book to come across your path for such a time as this. Nothing catches Him by surprise. Trust Him. He is the most beautiful Person who loves you dearly and wants to see you become all you can be in Christ. He truly is the One who sets you Free! He truly is the Way-Maker, whether you have the strength to believe it right now or not. He is the answer!

My hope is that someone who reads my book, or even a portion of it, will be inspired by my story and subsequent fight out of that place enough to decide not to give up; AND will find the stepping stones they need to walk out into freedom and victory for themselves and those they influence. That will give me the greatest delight. If He can do it for me, He can do it for you – get ready to leave those ruts for good!

## Testimonials

Kelly, a home educator and business partner, says:

*"About five years ago I was at the lowest point in my life. We had not only lost our business but were in the process of losing our home.*

*Throughout my life, I had battled with anxiety, fear and a need to be in control. During this time, while I was seemingly able to deal with these bigger issues, it was a lack of control in the smaller things that was causing the anxiety to get out of control. Things I hadn't dealt with in the past started resurfacing, and I felt myself spiralling down a dark hole that I just could not get out of.*

*I had been a Christian for most of my life, but I was struggling with surrendering completely to God, as I didn't completely trust that He had good intentions for my life. During this time, Annette came alongside me and kept pointing me to Jesus. Knowing that she understood the place where I was and knew how to get out the other side is without a doubt what helped me get to that place of freedom.*

*One of the Scriptures that she gave me that I held on to was Isaiah 26:3 - "You will keep in perfect peace those whose minds are steadfast because they trust in you." That Scripture proved so true, in the moments that my thoughts were completely fixed on Jesus, I had that perfect peace that the Bible talks about.*

*It was only when I would take my focus off Him and onto myself that I struggled. Annette showed me that my issue was my mind. It was such a revelation to me that I didn't have to think every thought that popped into my brain, that I could take 'every thought captive' and replace the negative ones with Biblical truths.*

*I will always remember her telling me that it would be a fight to get out of that place I was in and that I couldn't be complacent with my thinking. I couldn't just hope to get better. I had to get to the point where I stopped looking for anything but Jesus as being the solution and throw myself on the Word of God.*

*"Believe you can, or believe you can't, either way you will be right." She showed me that there is so much power in the words we speak and to choose to speak life over my circumstances.*

*Annette showed the importance of disciplining my thinking, suffocating the negative and replacing it with positive. It was a journey, but one I'm so grateful for.*

*My relationship with Jesus is so much stronger now. The tools Annette gave me are now just part of who I am. Everyone comments on what a positive person I am, how bright and bubbly I am. It's not that I don't have tough days; we all do, but my fallback is Jesus now. I know who to run to, and I'm careful about not letting complacency in, thinking I can do things in my own strength. I know I need Jesus every moment of the day and I'm now grateful to be able to surrender my life to the One who loves me perfectly. I can do and face all things through Him who gives me strength.*

*Thank you so much, Annette. I am so grateful, not just to God, but to you for not giving up on me, for loving me through it and seeing potential in me when I couldn't see it myself. I now use the tools that you showed me to help others. Life-changing!! "*

Fallon, a young mother and hairdresser, previously a positive and bubbly person, found herself in the darkest place of her life after a host of issues began surfacing, particularly after a most tragic and traumatic event imaginable.

Though she had plenty of mental health support, she was also a wonderful woman of faith and had a deep personal relationship with her God. She knew that ultimately it was God who had the answers. She would live in the Word and go well for periods, but then find herself back in this desperate, debilitating and dangerous place, hugely affecting her business, her family, her marriage and her life.

Her friend suggested she contact me, and I am just so grateful that she was so hungry and eager to put into practice the faith steps and cling to the Word of God for dear life. The Word works! And there is hope for even the hardest situations. Fallon is living proof. Fallon says:

*"I feel truly blessed to have had the amazing opportunity of being so encouraged at such a critical stage of my life by this incredible woman's journey to wellness. To know that she too had been to the darkest and most terrifying place really comforted me. I knew that if she pushed through, pierced through the darkness, I would be able to by His Mighty Strength.*

*Annette taught me to shift my focus onto Him every time I was consumed by what I thought would destroy me. Instead, I'd bring it to the feet of Jesus and 'look full in His wonderful face, and the things on earth would grow strangely dim in the light of His glory and grace'.*

*Thank you, Annette, for showing me His wonderful grace through your journey."*

Fran, a young mum of a one-year-old, soccer player and running enthusiast, joined our church at a critical and desperate time in her life when her baby was just four months old. When I visited her as a new Christian, she already had faith Scriptures posted all around her house and was hanging onto them for dear life. She was already a woman of faith, feeding on the Word, knowing God was her answer. She just needed that encouragement from someone who had been there, to help her persevere, rise up and fight, know she was on the right track and would eventually come out the other side and win. She says:

*"Annette was a huge support and help to me after I had my baby and got post-natal anxiety. She made herself available for me to talk to and was loving and patient with me through my worst times, always helping me to focus on right thinking and winning that battle in my mind.*

*Thank you, Annette, I was so blessed to have you there for me!"*

# PART ONE
# MY STORY

# CHAPTER 1
# AN IDYLLIC CHILDHOOD?

My family were prosperous, second-generation dairy farmers on a farm situated next to a typically small New Zealand town called Ohaupo, in the Waikato region. Both my parents had come from dairy farming backgrounds and built a brand-new brick home (brick was the newest style for their generation) during their first year of marriage.

Life very much revolved around the local community, school, church and farming activities. Almost everyone went to church, either Roman Catholic, Protestant or the occasional Jehovah's Witness.

Farming was hard work, and my dad worked in with my uncles who farmed nearby when it came to the big jobs, haymaking and rabbit-shooting. These were the less-hurried days of no television, mobile phones or internet, and the days of shared phone lines with your neighbours (called "party lines").

Our farmhouse was on the ridge that carried the main road, with a view looking out over our hen house and fruit orchard in the foreground, then beyond to the cowshed and farm sprawled below on the flat. It was on the corner of a metal, no-exit road (the one I learned to ride my bike down and have scars to prove it) which went downhill to the flat, servicing our farm and leading to the homes and farms of three other families, including a strawberry farm and mushroom factory.

My dad farmed both sides of this country road in some places, and the land on the right side backed onto a sizeable lake. It was an established and very profitable dairy farm, which allowed my parents to regularly purchase the latest new cars and farm machinery, as well as updating and improving our house and parklike grounds. My dad would occasionally acquire new land and expand his farming enterprise.

We lived about five minutes bike ride from our local village and were about 1.5 miles from our primary school, situated on the north side of our village. We walked to school, 1.5 miles there and back every day, mostly barefoot. My parents were considered well-to-do and upstanding in the community.

I was the second child, a daughter with three brothers. My dad's family hadn't had any girls for a few generations, so apparently were very chuffed to have a girl.

We very seldom took holidays; work was a high priority. There is only one "sort of" family holiday I can remember when I was 13 years old, where four of us did a tour of the South Island over a two-week period. In my later teen years, however, my parents purchased a holiday house at the beach, and that became a regular getaway, even if it was most often just mum and some of us kids.

## Keeping Up Appearances

I was brought up in a "church-going" home (we went to church, but there was no relationship with Christ), with a very strict childhood and was painfully shy. I found it difficult to make friends and can remember being very lonely.

My mother was a cruel disciplinarian, and I developed a real fear of her. She continually yelled and picked holes in me, and I always felt like I never measured up and that I could never please her. She was a perfectionist about everything in her life; her housework, her cooking, her entertaining, her appearance, her gardens, and what people thought of her. In our house, keeping up appearances was the norm.

My mother cared almost to the point of paranoia about what other people thought of her. If we ever passed on anything that a family member or someone else had said about her, she made a huge deal about it, interrogating us for every minute detail and continued to be almost irrational about it for weeks after. She seemed to have a delusional grandeur about herself, including her looks, and would constantly share any compliments people made about her.

Whenever my grandparents came to visit, or we were going to visit them in a nearby town, there was a list of all the things we were not allowed to tell them. We were sworn to secrecy on so many things; we were almost too scared to speak.

I had a good relationship with my grandma (on my mother's side) right up until she died. Her husband, Pop, died when I was 20, not long before my wedding, so in her later years, my grandma lived by herself and was relaxed, very homely and lovely.

My pop never said much, with his strong Irish drawl (mostly because we couldn't understand him). He just smoked away on his pipe or hand-rolled tobacco and smelt quite strongly of whiskey. He was kind enough to us kids and would tease or trick us sometimes.

Two or three times as kids, one of my brothers and I would stay with them for a few days in the school holidays. Grandma was very creative, always making something, and she taught me to knit, crochet, and make pancakes. I am sure she knew what my mother was like and was on the receiving end of her enough times, but she never discussed it with me. I remember her introducing me to her friends at her Presbyterian Women's Meeting one time, and she called me "dear". That was the first and only time I had ever been called by an affectionate term, and it really struck me so much that I have remembered it to this day.

My grandparents on my dad's side lived right next door. My grandad died while I was a baby, and mum had absolutely no time for her mother-in-law. I know they lived with them for the first year of their marriage, while their new house was being built. I don't remember much of this grandma, except that she was a bossy old thing. I remember mum arranging for her to be placed in a mental hospital when I was quite young because she apparently had dementia.

I was one of those kids with ears that stuck out, and mum always made such a big deal about them. I'm sure they grew twice as big because of all the times she yanked on them, sometimes tugging so hard she tore them at the top, telling me to cover up those "jolly" ears. Being such a perfectionist, she made such a big thing about them that I developed quite a complex until she made me have them operated on by a plastic surgeon in my teens.

I would have been about 17 at the time, as it was my first year working, and she made me pay for the plastic surgery. She was so worried about what everyone thought all the time, that no one could know about the operation.

When I came home from the private hospital, my head was bandaged all over like a helmet with just my face showing, and I bled a lot. I had to be holed up at home, with her living in fear of anyone coming and seeing me like this.

One of those days, to her horror, my grandparents decided to pay a visit. She hid me, making me lie under the spare single bed in my bedroom all day, petrified that they would see me and find out about the operation. Here I was, lying stiff as a board with my head fully bandaged on the hard floor, no room for a pillow, no room to turn let alone breathe and my nose touching the base of the bed. I had to stay that way for most of the day, long hour after hour, until they left. They would have assumed I was at work.

My mother also criticised the way we walked, making my elder brother and I walk up and down the path, head high, shoulders back, lifting knees, feet straight ahead, marching… no turned-in feet in this household… standing over us like a sergeant major. She criticised the way I ran, the way I held my head, the way I did my hair, and anything I said.

The result of this perfectionism meant that I became a very jumpy, nervous child. I wet my pants a lot, and as I grew older, withdrew from trying many things for fear of criticism. I was very aware that I didn't fit into my mother's world of perfection.

She would pounce on us kids for even the littlest thing, like accidentally dropping something, meaning I spent most of the time worried about making a mistake.

I did reasonably well at primary school in my younger years, but my parents didn't attend any annual school sports days or special events at school. I always had to find another family to sit with for lunch with my lunchbox, or find another loner to eat my lunch with on those days. No class photos were important enough to order.

Sometimes we would go to church socials, where everyone sat around the edge of the hall. They would have games for the children in the middle and all be cheering them on. I would be pushed or dragged to join in, but I was so painfully shy, I couldn't stand people looking at me and wouldn't budge off my chair. I would wish the floor would open up and swallow me. I was constantly told I wasn't allowed to do so many things, a lot of them out of my mother's fear. But then I also got in trouble when I was too fearful of having a go at something because I was "embarrassing".

I used to cry myself to sleep many nights because I felt so wretched and like I was never good enough. I've told myself over the years that my mother must have loved us four kids, but she just didn't know how to show it. She never did show it, not to me anyway – no cuddles or hugs or praise or loving gestures. Ever. The way she treated us was very cold. Things always seemed to matter more than people.

# CHAPTER 2
# CONTROL, MANIPULATION AND ABUSE

Along with this strong demand for perfectionism throughout my childhood, my mother also brought a very strong spirit of control and manipulation.

My bedroom needed to be perfect because anyone who came into the hallway to use the toilet could see down the hall into my room. The bedcover had to look just right. The bed was made (perfectly without a wrinkle) first thing in the morning, with the eiderdown plumped and placed "just so" on the end of the bed. I wasn't allowed to sit on or lie on the bed during the day to crease it, nor hang out in my room during the day.

Everything was kept like a showroom. The door was always kept open, even during the night, so I had no privacy, even as a teenager and young adult. The drawers were filled with my mother's things; I had just one for myself. I had a small shadow box on the wall with a few little trinkets, but otherwise, both wardrobes were also filled with her things, with a small space for some of my clothes and shoes. There was a cane vintage dolls pram in the corner, and a doll that she had purchased off her sister, but it was just for looks, not for playing with.

All toys and books were kept up high or put away, only to look at, not to play with. The only toys were outside ones such as bikes. It was basically her room that I was allowed to use for sleeping and dressing.

This blows me away now, with my four daughters all decorating and enjoying their rooms as they grew up, enjoying their private, lovely space with all their precious belongings. It was their sanctuary, and they loved their rooms over the years. They could never believe me when I told them what it was like for me.

There was other strange and manipulative behaviour. We were yelled at if we used too much toilet paper, and she started to mete out just one square for us each time. I had to ask her for every single sanitary pad, EVERY time. Right into my late teens. I kid you not! She would always make it difficult, just so she could use it as a form of control.

If I ever asked for anything or showed any love for something, it would be used as a source of manipulation and control. I remember something as simple as needing a colourful cooking picture for the front of my exercise book for cooking class at school. The one I really liked and chose from a magazine, my mother used on numerous occasions over several months as manipulation and control, to take off me and put up in the cupboard. My teacher was constantly on my case as to why I wasn't doing what she had asked and where it was, but I never did get to use that picture.

Mum sure taught us how to work! My three brothers would regularly escape down to the farm with my dad, so as the only girl, I was the one left at home to do the chores. Funny how my brothers would just disappear conveniently when there were chores to do!

Most Saturdays, I was on my hands and knees scrubbing the concrete on the back path and under the tank-stand (where everyone kept their farm boots). Walking home from school in the afternoons, I could often see in the distance large piles of weeds, branches and garden waste around the huge parklike grounds, and knew immediately what I would be doing until bedtime... cleaning it all up and carting it to the compost heap! If I dilly-dallied, it was more than my life was worth.

I have to say, Mum's gardens were something to behold; so perfect, so colourful and so parklike. They were her pride and joy and everyone commented on them. My dad was very good at creating limestone block or patterned block walls, fences, retained walls, edgings, paths and banks, plus wrought iron railings or fencing.

A regular chore during the summer was watering the large rose beds and picking all the rose petals and leaves off the scoria gardens underneath them, a massive job. Many of those chores including weeding gardens and holding the watering hose on the roses for long periods in the evening, I didn't mind doing because it kept me outside, away from Mum's disapproving glare.

My dad often wanted me to go over to the farm with him, but I wasn't allowed to, except on errands. Once, when I had to take a message to him on my bike, he wanted me to stay and learn to drive the tractor. I begged him not to because I knew I would get into trouble with Mum, but he was so keen to spend time with me, away from her controlling glare. That afternoon he taught me to drive the tractor down the farm race, but Mum could see from the house, and when I arrived home, I received a massive scolding.

It felt like my dad never stood up for me, just sniggering away in the background, thinking it was funny when we were told off. He liked to play and tickle us as kids and have a bit of fun, but as soon as we had any kind of fun with him, my mother would send us to bed. He never stood up for us, just gave in.

My mom would regularly hit me. I would miss school at times because of bruising and marks on my body from where she had beaten me in anger, yanked me, pulled my hair, slapped my face, wrung my wrists, grabbed me and dug her fingernails into my skin, or beat me with the wooden feather duster handle. Oh, I knew that solid feather duster rod well. It left some very deep and colourful stripes and deep bruising.

If we fought, as siblings do, her regular punishment was to bang our heads together. For some reason, I remember her holding my nose down on the hot toaster one day until it burnt. I ended up with a big blister, then scab, on the end of my nose and being kept home from school until it healed.

It was nothing for her to grab us in a head-hold and clean our teeth with "Vim" kitchen abrasive (similar to Jiff today) on the way out the door to church or somewhere special, because she decided our teeth weren't white enough.

Once I had forgotten to take my raincoat to school, so when I arrived home dripping wet, she stripped me down outside on the steps in the pouring rain and made me stand there in my underwear for half an hour. I was a teenager at the time. With my brothers around and feeling humiliated, I took off to hide somewhere. I didn't know where to go (in my underwear in the rain), so I hid in the dark, rat-infested firewood and potato shed.

When she found I was gone, I could hear her enlisting my brothers to hunt all over for me. They took up the challenge with glee, anything to get me caught and them in her good books. There was any number of places I could have been, but obviously I couldn't go far in my underwear. My eldest brother eventually found me quite a while later, and the discipline was even more brutal and punishing, and no dinner for me that night.

Due to this home environment of criticism, control and abuse (and regular silent treatment), I was very lonely and often used to get shut outside by myself with nowhere to go except sit under one of the cherry trees, lonely and dejected, or swing on the swing (but that was a little too close to the back door for comfort).

To this day, I still love flowering cherry trees. And I still love swings. Sometimes I played with the pegs in the peg basket and can remember sorting all the pegs into different groups.... the broken ones that needed mending, the dirty ones that needed cleaning, and the shiny colourful ones that everyone loved. I would pretend they were like people. Now, all these years later, I can see the beginning of my pastoral heart, way back then.

Some days my mother would shut me out of the house from early until late, and there were days on end she wouldn't talk to me; just a deathly silence and disgust wherever I went. In between these times, she would be angrily barking orders for me to do chores. I would creep in for mealtimes (if my dad and brothers were there) and creep in for bed.

My dad built a very nice concrete swimming pool, but it was away from the house, down by the cowshed because there were too many trees around the house and the leaves would be a problem in the pool.

Many days through the summer my family would pack a picnic basket full of food and beach towels and carry them down the metal road and along the tanker track to the pool, which was fenced and behind one of the hay barns. All the lounge chairs and pool equipment were kept in a dressing shed there.

On the days when my mother had shut me outside, I would often see mum locking the house and heading off down to the pool for the day, armed with food and drinks. She wouldn't say a thing to me; she just left, but if I wanted to be fed, I guessed that I had better follow. I don't think she cared whether I did or not. So, timidly and dejectedly, I would follow behind at a distance and creep through the gate for a bite to eat with the rest of my family when they arrived. With the others around, I wasn't so obvious.

Even when I grew older, my mum made all my decisions. She was always so uptight and had a very angry, controlling spirit. You never knew how she was going to be from one day or moment to the next, and I would end up creeping around the house to avoid being noticed by her in case I came into her line of fire.

In my teens, she started coming in while I was in the shower or bath and poking at me and criticising my body. There was such control, no privacy, it felt like emotional torture. Nothing was my own. Eventually, she made me shower outside as well and wash my hair outside in the tank-stand so that my hair wouldn't mess up her new shower.

There was a tall window in the tank-stand with no glass in it, right by the shower. The shower had no surround, just a showerhead and a soak hole in the corner of the concrete shed. I would try and block the open window with a hanging towel, and I could bolt the door from the inside, but it was very draughty in the winter. Thankfully it was milking time, and I was up early enough before my brothers were about.

The brick walls were dank and slimy, and the shed was filled with poisons and sprays and smelly jackets and gumboots. I would give myself a quick shower then wash my hair in the cracked hand-basin that was low down for the guys to wash their feet in. After always having to clean it first, of course.

The rest of the time, she would regularly tell me I was useless, I couldn't do anything right, I would never be any good, and never amount to anything… and I simply believed her. I hated myself and became shyer and shyer and further into myself.

Often, I used to consider suicide to end it all. On numerous occasions, I would find myself staring at those poisons in the tank-stand and try and work out how much I would need to take to do the job properly - anything to numb the pain and save me from this tyrant.

Unfortunately, I was also sexually abused during my childhood. I wasn't allowed to lock the door into the bathroom, even as a young teenager, and it was the only way through to the separate toilet. As I began to develop into puberty, the boys would find every opportunity to need to go to the toilet – one after the other. I was constantly trying to cover myself up in the bath until they had done what they needed to do. Any protests on my part just made it worse, and they would annoyingly hang around to see what they could see.

As I got older, my mother would make me dress in my bikini to do garden chores on the front lawn. I felt very exposed, but it gave her a strange pleasure to parade me on the main road like that. Today, I think, what on earth? It is probably no wonder that the older bachelor man who lived opposite us with his parents stalked me and creepily cornered me in his garage wanting to grope me, on more than one occasion.

Through those years also began many years of sexual harassment from a 30-year-old man who had worked for my father on the farm for about 13 years. He lived in a house out the back of ours.

As a young girl, I would have to clean his room and make his bed. I can remember it always stunk of cigarettes and who knows what else and there were pornographic magazines strewn around. Sometimes he would come in on me while I was cleaning it and I would try to escape quickly.

Over time, this escalated to where he would hound me, corner me, manipulate me, undress me and sexually abuse me, and I was too scared to do anything about it. Some of the things he put me through and made me watch were terrible, and a little girl should never have been subjected to.

Considering how controlling my mother was and how "nothing ever got past her" (truly, she had an eagle eye), he must have been so clever to seize his moments whenever she was out. He gave me a very expensive, beautiful doll as a bribe for keeping quiet. Being in his presence made me want to wretch.

The most difficult period, however, was when my brothers, and sometime later, my father, began to show a sexual interest in me, and sexually molested me. It was totally humiliating from my brothers, but I really trusted my dad in particular, so I was caught so unaware because you just don't expect that from your dad. He was a "so-called" fine, upstanding elder in the local church and even used to preach sometimes.

Due to mum's perfectionism, at one point when she was going away to our beach house, she decided she didn't want my father sleeping in their bedroom because she had just bought a brand-new bedspread and didn't want him messing it up. So, she told him he had to sleep in my room in the other single bed whenever she was away. It was so strange for her to do that when I think about it now as I was a teenage girl!

On those nights, he put so much pressure on me, playfully in the beginning, but then it progressed to much more than that.

Without going into details, I am so thankful to God that He protected me from rape, but it came very close. When you are young, you have no idea about these things, you are so naïve, and you just love and trust your dad. But even as a young girl I knew it felt strange and was not right. Even more than that, it was traumatic. I didn't want to go near him.

As our relationship changed, my mum picked up on it. She could tell something was different.

One day, she pinned me down until she got the truth. She hauled my dad in to discuss it, and I felt so ashamed, dirty and embarrassed for dobbing him in. She made me feel like it was all my fault.

There was never any apology, from either of them. Whatever was discussed behind closed doors, stayed behind closed doors, and it was never discussed ever again. But at least her control had put a stop to it. And my relationship with my father was never the same, ever again.

Due to this abuse, in particular from my family, I felt I had nobody I could trust, and I withdrew even more. My mum continued to hit me right up until the day I got married at 20 years old. I don't know how I came to stay at home that long. Just too incredibly shy and timid, I guess.

Looking back, I had no opinions and didn't know anything else, so I just accepted it all, while hating myself all the while. I probably presumed that was just normal too, to hate yourself. I was very withdrawn and had little idea of how other people lived and loved.

My life was so controlled and isolated (apart from church) that I just didn't know how things should have been. I had learned for so long that my feelings and opinions didn't matter anyway, that I had none. It was not until later years I started to question whether this kind of living and thinking was right.

## Are you there, God?

Throughout my childhood, I always believed in God. I remember talking to Him and telling Him my problems; He was the only one I had to talk to when I was so alone. But I didn't really know Him then, and I didn't even know if He cared. He was just a big God up in the sky somewhere. I had read the Bible stories at Sunday School and knew He existed, that was about all.

At times, I had tried to read through the Bible using a Bible reading plan, in a little tiny Gideon bible I had that was handed out at primary school. I did love that but didn't fully understand what I was reading. It made me feel closer to God somehow. I didn't know that I could have a relationship with Him.

When I was thirteen, along with a few others, I went through a Confirmation course and ceremony with my traditional church, confirming my christening as a baby and receiving a certificate to show that I was now presumably a fully-fledged church member. I had to memorize some passages and took it very seriously, even though I didn't understand it fully.

Other than that, I went along to church events with everyone else, including Sunday morning church services and Friday night Bible class, which was a social evening playing games with a handful of other youth from school. God was never talked about at home.

Years later, I realized that Jesus was never talked about as though He was alive at my church. Everything was always a memorial service to His previous death and burial and all that happened in the past.

I remember hard wooden pews with hymn books and hymn numbers, and getting the giggles when a regular church lady would trill really high and long every time we sang a certain line in "Onward Christian Soldiers". I remember the Harvest Festival Sundays where we filled the front of church with produce from our gardens and farms. I remember the Christmas plays where we often dressed as angels or sheep; the lead characters like Mary and Joseph were always reserved for the more confident kids.

I remember my mum teaching Sunday School for a period using the special flannel graph boards she had made, and many a church lunch in the back room after church. I remember saving used stamps off envelopes and taking them to church for the Leprosy Mission. I remember helping Mum do the church cleaning, vacuuming and floral arrangements twice a month when she was rostered on. And I remember the long drop out the back of church in a little wooden shed. It was the only toilet there was and smelt really bad. We would prefer to hold on rather than use it, but if necessity prevailed, we had to check for spiders first, then hold our nose while holding our pants up off the dirty ground before we sat down.

There were socials and weddings and funerals and christenings and all the usual church activities with mostly an older generation. That was church life for me. So, I always believed there was a God; I just didn't know Him… and didn't know that you COULD know Him. That was never taught, and I definitely would have heard it if it was. Deep down, I know I was searching for something more.

# CHAPTER 3
# GROWING UP AND FINDING MYSELF

As I GREW into a teenager, I did reasonably well at school, although I hated it. My mother had enrolled me in the professional stream at Melville High School, where along with the key subjects, I learnt French, possibly because of my French heritage on my father's side, and art (my favourite subject). I also loved music and playing the piano.

Music gave me a lot of satisfaction and was something I could get lost in; escaping the realities of my world. It was also something I could do well. Mum never minded me learning the piano, thankfully, and paid for my piano lessons for seven years. She would love it when I played for my grandparents.

My grandfather was Irish and loved me playing his favourite, "When Irish Eyes are Smiling". He would beg me to play tune after tune after tune. And somehow, my mum seemed to be proud of my piano playing; it was something she wished she had always pursued.

At age fifteen, I passed five School Certificate subjects, and then left school to do a secretarial course at Waikato Technical Institute (WTI) at my mother's directive, where I sat and passed two more School Certificate subjects. There I learnt accounting, typing and shorthand, and soon after, got a job working in one of the major banks in the city.

Again, it was through her accountant, who had a brother who was a bank manager, that she arranged the interview.

I started out as a teller and quickly progressed to becoming the Manager's Secretary. Although my boss was very strict and nobody else could work for him (his staff would only last a few weeks or days), he was a Christian and very good to me. He gave me praise and encouragement and often told me he really loved my work. And I really loved my work too, often willingly doing overtime when there were deadlines to meet. He was a tough boss, but I was used to that, so we seemed to gel somehow.

I began to gain a little confidence and self-worth in those years out in the workforce, although always hating to go home from work in the evenings. I would wait in the staff locker room so I could catch the very last bus possible. Mum just thought I was working late.

## Love blooms

Because a lot of her friends' daughters were having weddings, and "keeping up appearances" meant it wouldn't do to have an unmarried (spinster) daughter hanging around home for too long, my mother started trying to get me and my brother "out there" to Young Farmers Club and Saturday old-time dances, hoping I might meet a wealthy young farmer. She was very critical of those who were "left on the shelf". There was something wrong with them.

I didn't mind going along to the dances every Saturday night as I loved to dance; everything from foxtrots, waltzes, cha-cha's and maxinas, to Scottish dances such as the Gay Gordons and Strip the Willow. I never lacked for dance partners, and my brother and I even took a few ballroom dancing lessons. We both thrived in that environment.

It was at one of these earlier country dances with my whole family, that I met Ian, and he asked me out. The rule was that I could hang out with guys in a social setting or they could come home to our house, but I wasn't allowed to date until I was seventeen years old, but Mum seemed to like Ian, and let me join his family at a restaurant to celebrate his mum's birthday when I was just 16.

A couple of weeks later, he asked me to go to his Methodist Ball with him, and she agreed. He was painfully shy and looked like he wouldn't hurt a fly. I think my mother thought she would be able to manipulate him and boss him around, as well as the fact that he was from good "farming stock".

He was my first proper date ever, but so painfully shy and awkward, and now that I was finally allowed to date, I wanted to see who else may possibly be "out there". I'm sorry to say I broke his heart when I broke off our relationship after only a short time together, telling him I would like to be able to date other guys.

I had several interested suitors (at the dances, from work and from Young Farmers Club) who never passed my mother's approval because they were Catholic. With her strongly Protestant Irish father, that just wouldn't do! And she made it clear in no uncertain terms.

The first thing I had to do when I dated them was to find out if they were Catholic. My mother stood over me, threatening to do it herself until I broke it off with some of the nicest guys. I always had a strict curfew, home by 10.00 pm, and my brother was regularly sent along as the chaperone.

My relationship with Ian had been off for a period of about eight months, when she was actually the one who hooked us up again by phoning him and inviting him to a Young Farmers Club tractor driving competition that was being held on my dad's farm. He arrived in his flash new V8 Holden Kingswood (ex-Commonwealth Games car with blue and white stripes down the side) and took me for a ride in it. How could I resist?

Once we were back together, I received a last-minute invitation to his younger sister's wedding. He looked absolutely dashing as a groomsman in his suit and bowtie, and that night I fell head over heels in love.

We were allowed one date a week and one phone call a week (no mobile phones then), and she would be listening in constantly or sending my brothers to push through the door several times when she thought we should be hanging up.

Whenever he was able to come and visit on a Sunday afternoon, we had to sit bolt upright on the window seat in the dining area, not touching, along with all the rest of the family. Often the television would be on, and there would be little interaction between any of us. It felt so formal and awkward. I still to this day, don't know how Ian put up with it.

My mum knew exactly where we were at all times, knew exactly when the movies finished, knew exactly how many minutes it took to drive home after, and would always be waiting up. If I took too long in the car before coming in, I was rigorously scolded and duly punished.

One Saturday shortly after his sister's wedding, we drove to Morrinsville to help his sister and brother-in-law who were moving onto a new share-milking farm. It was such a fun day enjoying the outdoors and sunshine together, and that night while driving home, Ian asked me if I would marry him. He didn't stop the car or get down on one knee or anything, just continued on driving as though it was part of the conversation! Of course, I said yes.

When Ian eventually plucked up the courage to ask my parents if he could marry their daughter, they said "no"! Again, more as a form of control from my mother, but when she got thinking about it further, she realized that if it was going to happen, it would need to be in the autumn when cows were dry (not milking), and they would need to book a wedding venue and caterer probably a year in advance, and so they came back about three months later and said it would be ok for us to get engaged. She had checked out his parents' farm and the local traditional church he was part of.

By now it was August, and we were over the moon, to say the least. I was allowed to take the day off work, and Ian took me shopping for a ring.

We had the most amazing day, lost in love and dreaming of being together forever. He told me I could have any ring I wanted; price didn't matter. I truly couldn't believe it. But I didn't go wild with that offer, choosing a lovely diamond solitaire ring, a matching engagement and wedding ring set, which I still love to this day.

When we arrived home, my mother was very angry about the fact that we had bought a wedding ring, even though it would be put away until the wedding (of course).

We went to see Ian's parents to show them the ring, and they were so excited about it all - a real contrast.

Again, when I got home, Mum was angry that I stayed at Ian's parents' house too long. Even though I was over-the-moon happy, I could never show it around her.

My mum had chosen to celebrate our 20th birthdays (instead of a 21st), and my 20th was coming up four months later, in December. We had a combined birthday and engagement party in a local hall, with all her friends invited.

Sadly, my lovely Pop died a few days before, and that definitely put a damper on things, but we went ahead with it before the funeral, and Mum did all the catering herself.

It was a huge amount of work for her, and I remember her making at least eight of her huge pavlovas with massive fruit salads, large platters of ham and chicken and massive bowls of her favourite bean salad and curried rice salad. She had ladies from church lined up to work in the kitchen, but it still must have been a mammoth task. Mum was well-known for her phenomenal high rise, light and airy sponges, her cherry slice, savoury eggs, asparagus rolls and sponge fingers. She made a huge floral arrangement and arranged a pianist for the dance.

We were blessed with so many lovely engagement gifts that night, and people came from all over. Even though relatives were still grieving the loss of my Pop, it was a happy occasion. Our engagement gifts were all laid out in the lounge at home for several days, and many of her friends and our family came to view them. That was quite the socially acceptable thing to do then and quite the community occasion.

Then came the kitchen evening (as it was called back then) with all the men invited too. Another big event put on by my bridesmaids' families and so many lovely gifts from people leading up to the wedding in May. Wedding gifts started arriving early, and they were laid out in the lounge for people to view.

My mother's control was still in evidence, however, and on my wedding day she refused to talk to me the whole day. She had wanted a wedding card read out with the telegrams, and I wasn't so sure whether to or not. Her behaviour was always over something very trivial like this, and it was much easier to just go along with her or she made life so miserable. Even as an adult, if I showed any excitement about anything, she would use it as a punishment.

I had very little say over the wedding day. She chose the flowers (I wasn't even able to see them when my dad picked them up from the florist); she chose the hairdresser and the hairstyles. She chose the bridesmaids, their dress material and style, plus the dressmaker. The wedding gown she chose for me, I didn't like the pointy bodice, and with the support of the bridal salon ladies, they helped me exert my influence to choose the one I really did like. This one I was paying for.

She came with us for the groom and groomsmen (one of them my elder brother) to get their suits and chose them all, right down to the shoes, insisting they were to get their hair cut and wear "tight undies" on the day. The groom and his family weren't even allowed to know where the venue was until they received their wedding invitations six weeks out from the wedding!

One great thing about my mother controlling every detail of my wedding is I had a fairly carefree day and didn't have to worry about a thing. It wasn't a cheap wedding, being the only daughter, and everything had to look just perfect. I never knew all the details; those were just decided for us.

After the reception and dance, we slipped away upstairs to get changed into our "going away outfits" (as they were called back then). Our bags were already in the hotel room, and we were sent upstairs to quickly get changed and return to the guests dancing downstairs. Imagine our surprise moments later when she sent my father up to bang on the door and ask us where we had got to. I kid you not.

After 20 years of emotional and physical abuse, I left home to start a new life with my wonderful new husband. Even that wasn't without its control. My mother was so annoyed that Ian hadn't told her where we were going on our honeymoon (back then, couples used to keep it as a surprise, as friends had been known to gate crash). She was angry because we were late getting to her house the morning after the wedding, our first honeymoon night. She had a houseful of friends and family over for lunch and a cup of tea, and I was instantly ordered into the kitchen to work. She was angry because we flew out of the country to Norfolk Island for a week (the "in" place for a honeymoon at that time), and so angry that we stayed a night in Auckland with Ian's aunty and uncle on our return home. She insisted that we weren't allowed to go to our new home straight away but had to stay at her house until late. We weren't even allowed to take our wedding presents home until the next day; they were all on display in her lounge. And can you believe she told me that I was walking differently after our honeymoon? I mean, who does that?

I had finished work in the week preceding our wedding, receiving an amazing farewell and reference from my boss. Moving to the country onto my new husband's farm meant that it would be too far to travel to work, and besides, I would have plenty to keep me occupied.

# CHAPTER 4
# GOD IS THE BEST MATCHMAKER

When I met Ian, he taught me how to love. My background of never feeling good enough, and of never receiving the nurture or affection I needed, along with the abuse throughout my childhood had meant that I had no idea what real and true love was. Ian showed me that.

I'd been out with other guys, but they all had one-tracked minds, and I didn't want a bar of it. I wanted to wait for marriage. It's a wonder I didn't turn right off men, but Ian was different. He loved me for me. He spoilt me. Nothing was ever too much for his girl. I had never had someone love me like that. I continually praise God for giving me such a kind, understanding man, exactly what I needed, and he has been a huge part of my healing.

When you are a child, you just think your home is normal; it is your only benchmark. You don't question that perhaps other families live differently. This was my case in particular as we were so isolated.

I was seldom allowed to have friends around to our place or go to others' houses to play. There are only two friends' houses I can remember visiting, and their mothers were strikingly loving and kind; I remember being blown away by it. And it was a huge mission to persuade my mum to let me have a friend come over, but I didn't enjoy it anyway because what few toys we had were always put away up high, not for playing with, and that was embarrassing to explain to friends. They would always want to play in my bedroom, but we weren't allowed in there.

And while they were there, my mother would find a way to scold and put me down in front of them or cause division between myself and my friends, ganging up against me, picking on me with them. It really wasn't until I started sharing a few things with my husband, and he was so incredulous at what he heard, that I started to realize how controlling and abusive my upbringing really was.

After only two weeks into marriage, Ian became aware of how much I loved cats. We looked up the adverts in the local Waikato Times, and there was a Blue Persian cat for sale locally. He said, "Why don't we go and get it?"

I remember being so shocked and replied, "Really? Right now? We can go, just like that?" I felt like I needed to ask my mother's permission first, and I couldn't believe that I could make this decision without a huge rigmarole to get something I would love. Ian just wanted to see me blessed, no conditions, no reluctance, and we went straight away to bring home this gorgeous little kitten which I loved. And it was even more special because he had bought it for me.

Ian had a really caring family, and we were blissfully happy. His parents had previously moved out of the main farmhouse into the farm cottage across the paddock before our wedding. They were happy to make way for us, without any issues. Ian always laughs that "they moved out and I moved in". He just stayed in the same house, which we updated, refurbished and made ours.

As time went by, we bought the farm off his dad and began a family. We continued to go to church each Sunday but began to drop away a bit, because it felt dead and boring and no other young people attended. We were very involved in the local Young Farmers Club, travelling all over the countryside to the competitions and gatherings they had on and had heaps of great friends.

In our early years of marriage, I still had a lot of interference from my mother. She criticised everything we did and everything we bought. Often, she would ask how much things cost then go and buy herself a better or more expensive version. She had previously stipulated that Ian had to bring me home to visit her every Sunday afternoon. She always criticised him (the way he walked, the way he spoke, the way he held himself), and would have happily broken our marriage up so she could have more control back. She tried to make me feel guilty by saying that if I hadn't married Ian, I could be coming on their luxury cruise ship holidays with them.

At one stage before our marriage, she was very critical of his speech; the fact that sometimes he would use "f" or "v" instead of "th" in his words. I was mortified, as she insisted that before I could marry him, I had to bring it up with him and get him to change the way he spoke! There was no way I wanted to do that, but she kept on about it so long that eventually I had to, or the marriage would be off. I was so embarrassed when I shyly brought it up one night when we were out to the movies together. The poor guy even had a nasty cold, and I stumbled over the words to say, ever so kindly, that my mum had this issue with his speech. He was just so amazing about it, saying that no one had ever brought it to his attention before, and from that day on, he changed and never spoke like that again. I could tell it was a big deal for him, and often would catch him carefully choosing a word before he spoke it. What a honey, to have to put up with all that just to have me!

I didn't realize it in those early years, but I had gone into marriage with a lot of problems just covered over, which were to surface in later years of pressure. We never had a single argument in our first year of marriage... at least not until our first baby came along. We were madly in love and keen to start a family as soon as possible, discovering we were pregnant only three months into our marriage.

Mum's shocked response when we broke the news was, "For goodness sake! You could have waited a bit longer. People will think you were pregnant before you were married!" But we were over the moon and keen to have a good-sized family, determined to build a home far different than what I grew up in.

After our first darling daughter was born, my mother tried to destroy our excitement. She continually criticised us. She was angry that Ian hadn't called her sooner to let her know the baby had arrived (no mobile phones back then). He, in his naivety, was waiting for nurses to weigh the baby so he could tell her what the weight was when he called her. She didn't like the names we chose and insisted they be changed. One of the names was too "Catholic" and the other had to be the full version, not the shortened version we liked. So instead of Jenny Maree, within a few short hours she had to become Jennifer Louise (Louisa being my mother's second name, but I dropped the "a" on the end without her knowing).

My favourite uncle (her younger brother) died at age 33 while I was still in the maternity hospital with our first daughter. My mum even called the matron and insisted I not be allowed out for the funeral. Then she didn't want me to go home with the baby because she was jealous of Ian's mum (who lived across the paddock). She put a lot of pressure on me to go back to her place. Yeah right! Not this time.

She was there at my house when we arrived home and caused trouble at every turn. I was always so stressed with her around. She was constantly jealous of Ian's mum who lived close by, having any contact with the baby, but it felt like that wasn't coming from love for her first grandchild, but rather a sense of control. I never found her cuddling or cooing over our little girl, just wanting to exert her control, pose for photos and stamp her ownership on the situation above Ian's mother. I couldn't even enjoy my own baby in her presence, as she stood off in judgment or belittling everything I did.

When our daughter was just four months old, I was admitted to hospital with acute appendicitis, needing an operation to remove my appendix. Ian was very good with the baby, so he took her home to his parents to stay. He would look after her, but his parents would have her while he needed to attend to farm duties. That absolutely infuriated my mum who, instead of showing any concern for me, was just jealous over who had the baby. She insisted that Ian had to bring me back to her house with the baby as soon as I was discharged from hospital. I lasted there for a couple of days before I couldn't wait to go home.

I'm sorry to say I would get frustrated with my baby when she would do something trivial that my mother wouldn't approve of. She didn't think I was disciplining her enough and kept telling me the baby was "highly strung". For example, not saying "ta" (aka "thank you") when reaching out for something as young as six months deserved a smack on the hand according to her. As a first-born daughter, she was very determined, and I found myself becoming uptight and overly strict on her, all because she'd done something trivial my controlling mother wouldn't have approved of. I would get stressed when I knew my mother was coming to visit and would race around the house, making sure it was not only clean but spotless.

As time went on and we had more children, she began pointing out their physical imperfections and picking holes in them. She also started comparing them, preferring one above the other and doting on the one she thought was the prettiest. If things had continued this way, I shudder to think what could have happened to our children.

## Joy Unspeakable

Thankfully, four years into our marriage, we came to know Jesus Christ through the witness of some friends (who incidentally prayed for us and didn't give up on inviting us to meetings). We got tired of their pestering and had run out of excuses to say no, eventually agreeing to get them off our backs. Praise God for those Christians who don't give up – who keep going back and back even when they get knocked back!

Over a period of time, just between ourselves, we began to realize we were just "church attenders" and were not really Christians at all, and so one day, the two of us knelt in our dining room together and said, "God, if you are really real, then we ask you to come into our lives and reveal yourself to us, whether you are really real or not."

He sure did! One of the songs around at that time was "Joy Unspeakable and Full of Glory". We played it loud throughout our house. It really couldn't describe our experience more perfectly. We were on Cloud Nine!

I didn't tell my parents for a long time that we had become Christians. It was too precious to have them ridicule and stamp all over our decision. There would be plenty of time for that later on. By this time, we had our second gorgeous daughter. Life felt like a bed of roses, and God blessed our already blissful and flourishing marriage.

The traditional church we were a part of didn't even believe in salvation, let alone discipling, so we discipled ourselves. We frequented the local Christian bookshop, buying studies on knowing Jesus, and devoured them. We bought the latest music albums and filled our house with Gospel songs. We bought books on marriage and read up on how God viewed Christian marriage. We also fed ourselves with great books on God's plan for raising a family.

I am so thankful we found Jesus at this time, early in our marriage. Things were about to get very tough, as God brought my pain and abuse to the surface to be dealt with. I couldn't have walked through the next few years without Him.

# CHAPTER 5
# PRESSURE BRINGS "STUFF" TO THE SURFACE

EVEN THOUGH THERE were signs that my past was starting to bring up difficult thoughts and patterns of behaviour in me, things on the surface were going well as I headed into my third pregnancy. We believed everything was fine until devastating news hit – our baby had passed away in my womb at 29 weeks. The baby had died due to a rare hormonal disease; a one in 2000 rare condition and had to be removed through an operation in hospital.

Losing a baby at any time is devastating, but so far through the pregnancy is incredibly difficult. I came home to a nursery all ready for a little one. My milk had fully come in, but I had no baby!

The shock and suddenness of it all was so traumatic. I was just lost. I didn't know what to think or feel. Life went on for everyone else around me, yet here I was coping with the grief upon grief of losing someone so longed for and so loved, so part of me.

I never blamed God but had thoughts around maybe there must have been something wrong with the baby for it to die, and maybe that was better like that. All I could do was trust that He knew best.

This was all in our very first year as new Christians. I never saw the baby (they didn't allow that back then) and never knew what gender;

these things may have helped bring closure. I remember going away to stay with Ian's sister and family for a week or so, just to rest and recover, as everywhere I looked around my house, there were reminders we were expecting a baby.

For a long time after, I would keep seeing pregnant mothers or mums with babies and be reminded that that could be me; my baby could be around that age.

Following our loss, I had to undergo numerous blood tests and chest x-rays for several years, as the condition had a high rate of malignancy. I also kept bleeding non-stop for around 18 months. Specialists had told me I wasn't allowed to have any more children for two years, but I begged and begged them until eventually, they agreed to let me try for another baby. That's all I wanted.

Looking back, it is easy to see that it was not wise because I was so run down that I would have been better to have waited and got completely well again. I was still grieving the loss of my previous baby and thought having another would fix it all.

Again, trauma hit, I miscarried my next pregnancy once more, this time in the first trimester, then fairly quickly got pregnant again. I was over the moon. God had answered my desperate prayers. I remember promising Him, that if he would just give me another baby, I would gladly give it back to Him, like Hannah in the Bible. It was turning out to be a very eventful four-year gap between children, instead of the planned two years between them all, but so grateful to be once more adding to our gorgeous family.

Each time I plucked up the courage to tell my mum the happy news of these pregnancies, she would make a disapproving quip like, "For goodness sake, you're breeding like rabbits," or "Really? For God's sake, most people are only having two these days. That's a much more respectable number." I think I had long given up wishing she could be happy for me.

At six months pregnant, I was hit by a very bad flu virus, which took two full months to get over and regain some of my strength. On the farm, Ian was in the middle of calving, and I can remember really struggling with no help. To make it worse, a terrible whooping cough virus was going around, and the two girls got it (even though they had had their immunisations). It lasted for three long months! They coughed and coughed and gasped for air night after night, day after day.

I remember going to a school sports day near the end of it, and truly, without a lie, most of the children were coughing and whooping up and down the field as they ran. That is all you could hear!

I was very weak and rundown and found myself getting tenser and tenser, tied up tight like a rubber band. I had spells where I thought I was going mad, and the doctor put me on anti-anxiety pills. On the odd occasion, if my mum had phoned or I had phoned her, I would tell her I was not well with no energy. She never came to help; just said very matter-of-factly, "Oh, you'll manage," and then went on with all the stories of her life.

Around this time, my parents had handed over the running of their farm to my elder brother and his new wife. Unfortunately, I was not the only one who was hugely affected by my mother's behaviour. The control she exerted over my brother was terrible. She was obsessed with it in all her phone conversations with me.

She turned him against his wife using lies and manipulation, undermining his wife behind his back and eventually playing a large part in causing my brother's marriage to be destroyed in the years to come. He had so much pent-up anger inside of him, and his wife was regularly on the receiving end of it. She left and went into hiding with her children, eventually changing their surnames so they couldn't be found. They had four children, two of them twin boys.

My mother had always wanted twins herself, and one of the first things she did when their marriage was breaking up was tell me she was going to fight for custody of the twins. Not because she loved children, but because she loathed her daughter-in-law and wanted to get back at her.

In these days, having my new-found faith and gaining some confidence in what I believed, I would start to nicely but firmly challenge her on the phone when she was running down my sister-in-law or pouring out all her lies and manipulation. I didn't disagree outrightly, just started to stand up for my brother and sister-in-law. I was fair shaking as I did so.

She did not like that at all, and became very defensive, hanging up on me angrily. She would phone back wanting to know who was there, listening, egging me on, putting these words in my head. She was certain someone else was influencing me.

I became so tired of the ugly control and interference going on with my brother, and could finally see through it all, that this was the first time I had ever been able to pluck up the courage (shaking and all) to say anything. I just couldn't handle having to stand and listen to this constant barrage coming down the phone for hour after hour.

The last few weeks of my pregnancy were terrible. I was so weak, with no energy or strength. I had my longest and most painful labour on the hottest day of the year (no air con in those days), and after fourteen hours of strong, induced labour, my third daughter was born posterior.

I absolutely cherished my little blonde princess. She was perfect. She was everything I had dreamed of and more. I was delighted to finally have my third baby, but in the weeks to come, I became very depressed.

I felt extreme exhaustion, day after day was spent in tears just going through the motions of living, fluctuating from terrible panic, anxiety and fear to chronic depression, aching deep down inside. I could describe more, but some of you will know what I'm talking about.

This went on for eighteen long months. I considered suicide many times, just to end that revolting pit that I felt like I was being sucked down into. I wasn't sleeping at night; my mind was way too active, and I felt just seconds away from a panic attack constantly.

One wrong thought would send me spiralling downward. I lived in fear of those panic attacks because I couldn't trust them and didn't know what to do with them. I literally felt like I was losing my mind. It truly is the most terrifying place to be in!

Even though I adored Ian and the children (they were the lights in my life), I just couldn't see any point in living. I lost all interest in gardening, cooking, sewing, handcrafts – all the things I previously loved doing. I would pray to the Lord. Ian would pray and try to comfort me, but nothing worked. It was like living in hell inside.

I developed a real fear of being locked up, ending up in Tokanui Mental Hospital like they used to do, and that made things worse – knowing "the things that you fear can come upon you" (Job 3:25).

Night times were definitely the worst, and I dreaded them. I couldn't rest and was lucky to find three hours to sleep between waking up with anxiety and panic attacks. At least during the day, I had things to look at and focus on but there was this deathly sadness all day long. It was a living nightmare that I put up with each day, and it was incredibly exhausting.

I remember one night in particular (there were many) getting up and pacing, to try and get some solace from the darkness. I ended up on my hands and knees in the hallway, so afraid I was losing my mind, going mad. Ian called the duty doctor, and he told him to give me some Panadol!

Depression, anxiety, postnatal depression - none of this kind of thing was ever talked about back then. It had a real stigma about it. The medical profession was of little help. My doctor prescribed anti-depressants, but they made no difference. And if I had gone to my traditional church to ask for help, they wouldn't have had a clue to know what to do. There was no counselling as such for people in this situation. There was no internet or Google to help. The only books I could find were at the local Christian bookstore, and there were none on this subject. People just didn't talk about this kind of thing.

I tried everything I could do to break the shackles and end the constant barrage of spinning thoughts inside my head and that awful pit in the depths of my stomach which was trying hard to suck me down. Life was no longer enjoyable. My stomach was constantly sick, and I would regularly vomit or wretch from deep sadness, from deep within. All of that "stuff" was coming up from my childhood, and I had no idea what was happening to me.

I would beg Ian to take us away on holiday, and then when we got there, I couldn't sit still and would beg him to take us home because it felt safer. And then when I got home, it seemed to be full of depressing memories of trying to cope.

I tried reading up on what could be causing this and check in with my doctor every now and then to ask if there was something lacking in my system. He said, "No, no, no…a healthy young woman like yourself, eating a balanced diet, shouldn't have any problems". He finally suggested he could refer me to a psychiatrist, and I was terrified. NO way! They might lock me up and put me away.

If my mum found out, she would certainly want to, like she did her mother-in-law, to get rid of the shame. My mum would take my kids! And what a "hell" of a life they would have!

Surprisingly, when I look back, I actually kept up a reasonable face on the outside. Nobody would have known what I was going through and how desperate I was. I withdrew and wouldn't go out much. When I tried to share with anyone, I felt like they just made glib comments, and I realized no one really understood.

I felt so alone but couldn't stand crowds and would feel claustrophobic and have to get out (sometimes even in the supermarket). I also felt a real failure, ashamed that I wasn't coping well. I was fulfilling my mother's words to a 'T' – I WAS useless! She was right!

I loved my children to bits and looked after my baby and children well. I kept up the housework, but at times felt like I was just going through the motions. I had no one to help. Ian couldn't understand. He tried to. I'd always relied on him, but he couldn't get down inside and help me.

I had also contracted glandular fever when my baby was just six weeks old, and that lasted for months, but I struggled on. I had a Karitane nurse once a week come in and support me and check on me for about a month. I was not only totally rundown and suffering emotional exhaustion but was also physically very unwell. Many times, I wanted to end it all, and yet I had everything – I loved the Lord, I loved my husband and family. I had everything going for me. I was praying and reading my Bible. But I couldn't seem to "snap out of it" – there were things deep down inside that needed dealing with. This wasn't something that I could just take a pill or snap out of. I am so thankful God knew this and led me on a journey towards finding the tools I needed for my healing.

## Unwinding the Rubber Band

About that time, I read an advert in the local paper. A well-known Hamilton pastor of a large church was speaking on "How not to have a nervous breakdown" – it was just a tiny ad - so I phoned their office and ordered the tape. (Yes, cassette tapes back then!)

His teaching was the beginning of a breakthrough, and I started to see some light at the end of the tunnel. One of the things he mentioned was about Vitamin B being the nerve vitamin, so I got myself some and began taking them. I started to feel a bit stronger physically, reasonably quickly.

Another reassuring thing he said was that "your nerves can't break" – they just get all tensed up in knots, like a rubber band. He taught me to say, "So what!" instead of getting stressed and tied up in knots. "So what!" Those two words became my new favourite words. "So what" when the kids broke something! "So what" when the washing machine broke down! "So what" when they were all shouting at the same time. "So what" the weather was awful! "So what" when things didn't go to plan! "So what" if the kids were being naughty! "So what" if I heard a noise in the middle of the night! "So what" if I started to get stressed or fearful about something, as if I didn't care.

Another of his taped messages taught me to practice the presence of Christ. When I could stick to that, it really helped. And because of what he had mentioned about nerves being tied up tight like rubber bands, I started learning some relaxation techniques to unwind those tightly wound "rubber bands".

Because this man had two or three nervous breakdowns himself, he seemed to know what he was talking about. I didn't have a clue what the "label" was for what I was going through, but it really gave me hope. I eventually concluded that I had two choices - to give up and stay like this forever and live a life of hell (on the inside) or fight and have victory over it.

To take my mind off myself, and while nursing the baby and playing with the kids, I had been watching a television programme called "That's Incredible". I began to realise there was something in positive thinking. If people had enough determination, they could do just about anything! And they actually did! With sheer will power. Their achievements were phenomenal. Some even fought their way back out of alcoholism, losing their business, marriage and family. I was really taken by it. And I had God on my side, so together He and I could do it, surely! I had nothing else to lose. Faith began to come into my heart. I had also been reading some faith books and started to get some feistiness and indignation at what the devil had stolen from me. I wanted to make him pay!

One day I plucked up the courage to pray for healing again. It had been eighteen long months by this time, and I was so sick and tired of being sick and tired and chronically depressed, so I flushed all my pills down the loo, determining that I would let Jesus control my mind and thoughts. I was sick and tired of being messed up and tired. Sick and tired of battling fear and panic and that deep dark hell hole. Exhausted with it all. The thing is, I had been praying constantly for healing. I walked around and around in my bedroom, day after day, night after night, month after month begging God to heal me. I knelt, I cried, I bawled, I wailed, I worshipped, I begged. And I became increasingly distressed and frustrated because He wasn't taking it away. No amount of tears and prayers was making any difference. He wasn't healing me! How long, God, I would cry out? How long will you leave me like this? Don't you love me?

# PART TWO
# FAITH BEGINS TO DAWN

# CHAPTER 6
# CAN GOD'S WORD BE TRUSTED?

I WANT TO SHARE with you the key that helped me out of the pit. As I was reading these books and listening to these tapes, it began to dawn on me that perhaps I could trust God's Word.

As I was meditating on the Scriptures, the light suddenly started breaking in! I read that Jesus had already carried not only our sins, but also our sicknesses and diseases on the Cross of Calvary. Jesus had already healed me. The work was finished! Jesus had done His part. *"By His stripes I AM healed"* (present tense), and now what I had to do was appropriate that. To walk in it by faith. That was my part. It was such a shock revelation. The Word says that God healed ALL who were oppressed, not just SOME! Healing was mine by faith.

Faith began to really explode in me. I decided to begin to *"...call those things that were not as though they were..." (Romans 4:17)*. Here I was, all this time, begging for Him to heal me, and He was saying, "I have, Annette! Once and for all. I have already! It's all yours! Just reach out and receive it...by faith! You have to begin to receive it and confess it by faith, and then you will have it."

I came across a verse in the Bible that says, *"Thou will keep in perfect peace whose mind is stayed on Thee" (Isaiah 26:3)*. I determined to do just that and see if it was true or not. I thought I believed the Word of God, I really did. I loved the Word! But it is not until you begin to depend on it for dear life, that you find out whether you really do believe it or not!

"You mean to say, God, that if I keep my mind stayed on You, then you will keep my mind in perfect peace? Really? I can take that word literally? If that is the truth, I am going to throw myself on it, and You prove to me that it is true. I'm going to let go of everything else. I'm just going to throw myself on your Word. You prove it, God!"

And so I did, and without a lie, all the time that I kept my mind focused on Him, my mind was at peace. I was amazed! His Word really does work! And my faith began to grow even more.

It was not an easy discipline because my mind was up and down and all over the place and my physical and emotional self was also all over the place. It was very difficult and a lot of work to bring my mind into line constantly. It was a real fight! My mind didn't want to toe the line. I had to train it. I had to make it. And bearing in mind at this stage, I still had no proof, no guarantee that it would work. I had no one else guiding me. Just Him. I had to believe and trust. I had to take Him at His Word. I had nothing else to hang onto that was working. "God, you had better come through for me, or I am a lost cause completely."

## Becoming a Film Censor

I forced myself out of that pit. I fought my way out with the Holy Spirit's help. And the more I clung to His Word and believed it, the better I started to get. I had to cut any doubts out of my mind. I had to be like a film censor and censor out everything negative.

I repeated over and over, *"I can do all things through Christ who strengthens me." (Philippians 4:13)* I would repeat it as I tackled the daily chores and whatever else I needed to do. That verse came alive to me and is still my favourite today. Every time negative thoughts of self-pity or not being able to cope came along, I would cut them off immediately, so they had NO TIME to take root. I literally kept my mind stayed on Christ!

*"Fix your eyes on Jesus, the author and perfecter of your faith" (Hebrews 12:2)*. Fix, fix, fix, like super-glue! (my diary read). I absolutely refused to think about self. I got busy, making lists of things to do and goals to reach. I would leave my list in a prominent place on my kitchen bench and often, when I was still feeling terrible, with my thoughts wanting to go south, I would just begin the next thing on the list….and think nothing. There was great satisfaction ticking each of them off, but only after I had completed each one fully. It was a great motivator. I began to strive toward them and really pushed myself at times (believing I was healed by faith) because my body still didn't feel like it. I had to get my mind off myself and keep it off. I refused to think about how I felt because one thought would send me spiralling back into fear.

I disciplined my mind in this way over several months. It didn't happen instantly. I had to keep it up. I couldn't trust my feelings or thoughts at all. One wrong thought would send me skyrocketing into anxiety and fear.

2 Corinthians 10:5 tells us that we are to *"demolish arguments and every pretension that sets itself up against the knowledge of God, and **we take captive every thought** to make it obedient to Christ."* Our minds have something like 50,000 thoughts run through them every day (like, who counted them?)! Not every one of those thoughts is positive. In fact, a whole lot, if not most of them, are negative. I began to realize that I was a very negative person, especially after my negative upbringing. My brain needed re-programming. A whole lot of those negative thoughts had to be cut out. I learnt to just not give them a "second thought."

Thoughts can go through your mind, but you don't have to dwell on them. It was hard work. I saw the reel of thoughts going through my mind just like a movie reel and I had to edit the bad bits out, just like the film censors do.

*"…do not worry about tomorrow, for tomorrow will worry about itself.*
*Each day has enough trouble of its own."*
*(Matthew 6:34)*

I had to make my mind stay focused on Christ and walk completely by faith, even when all else seemed totally contradictory. As I really concentrated on this, one day at a time, it became a little easier.

On the bad days, I had to take just one minute at a time. I couldn't even think about the next hour, let alone the next day without all kinds of fears spiralling upwards because I didn't know how I was going to get through. I just had to focus on now. But I kept on pushing through and persevering, small step by small step.

By just taking one day at a time (or one minute) and refusing to think about the future or the next hour (and I really had to work at it), I was gradually healed by the power of the Word of God working in me. I was quoting Scripture after Scripture meditating on them throughout the day, picturing and imagining them going to work on healing my mind and body.

## God's Word is Living and Active!

There is power in the Word of God! IT WORKS! I've proved it time and time again since then. There is healing in the Word and it is the only book that has all the answers. As I quoted the Word of God, I saw it as living and active and working in and around my life, accomplishing what it said it would do. The Bible says, "it does not return void".

Through these trials, I developed a real strength in my faith. I could see and feel the Word of God working. No more doubts and fears. Jesus WAS really real – He had proved it. His Word IS truth! Wow!

# CHAPTER 7
# THE GREATEST COUNSELLOR IN THE WORLD

DURING THE TIME I was still on my journey back to wellness, we had started a youth ministry in our local country church. Amazing, when I think about it now. We met fortnightly on Sunday evenings at our house on the farm. Ian and I would travel all over the countryside picking the kids up and had around twenty regularly attending from all over our Ngutunui-Pirongia-Te Pahu region.

Our minister only wanted church kids to attend (of which there were about two), but we just kept on reaching out and gathering more in. We had some amazingly creative, hilarious and crazy times with them all, along with themed nights and Bible studies.

Our three girls joined us for everything, my youngest a toddler by then, including our youth camps. The youth loved them. At one of those camps, we joined with another youth group camping at Kaiaua on the Thames coast. We hired a campervan to help me look after the baby especially, during all the youth chaos and hi-jinks. Those were some very special times, and the beginning of our ministry.

When Hannah was just two years old, we all headed off on a family holiday together with Ian's sisters and their families. Driving down both the North Island and the South Island, we stayed in cabins and campgrounds along the way and arrived in time to spend Christmas with Ian's sister and family who were farming in Ashburton. On the way I remember 21 of us all walking down the main street in Timaru. It was lots of fun all travelling together and visiting other tourist spots like Dunedin and Queenstown.

During this time, only one more fear remained. Due to what had happened in my last pregnancy, I wanted no more pregnancies - no more babies for a long, long time. We put that decision of a fourth baby off to the future.

I began to feel good about myself again, and it was really neat to have defeated the enemy and be walking in victory. The Lord had showed me some things in the spirit in those times. I developed a great strength in my faith and was so much closer to God.

I was still careful. I had to stick close to Him because I needed Him so much for every step of the way. I learned to practise the presence of God daily and to have a Spirit-controlled temperament. No more drastic mood swings, and without any pills either! I leaned into Him to keep me on an even keel. (Note – please hear me here. I am in no way against medication (or counselling) for these issues, and I never encourage people to do what I did and flush medication down the toilet! I believe that was a gift of faith that God imparted into me, to do that. There are times when medication is needed to level you out or hold you steady because such an imbalance has taken place, and everything has got way out of kilter into a downward spiral. So, I praise God for the miracle He performed in my life because the medication wasn't working for me.)

I am so grateful to God because many go on to develop manic depression, bi-polar disorders, schizophrenia or other mental health issues. The more I thought of those, the more fear it only put in me. I don't profess to know all the ins and outs of mental health disorders, but what I do know is my mind was on a knife-edge, so incredibly fragile and wanting to spin way out-of-control. If I let it, it would speedily head towards a point of no return, into a deep, dark hole that would suck me into its out-of-control abyss.

I had been an absolute mess, shaking uncontrollably at times, but was now SO THANKFUL to be back to a place of peace and coping better with stress.

Hannah was nearing two years old by the time I realized I was having way more better days, than bad ones, and she began to thrive too. She never fed well, was constantly sleepy, and it took me hours to feed her as a newborn. It seemed like she didn't like milk at all, and quickly weaned herself off breastmilk and other kinds of milk. Although she was happy enough and growing, I was constantly concerned she wasn't getting the nutrition she needed. (Years later, I now wonder if she was Vitamin B deficient also, as I was. There were never any tests done.) So, when she began to really thrive from this time onward, it was a huge relief also.

Then, all of a sudden, I found I was pregnant again! I was in such shock that I jammed my finger in the car door when I popped out of the doctor's clinic to tell my husband the results of the test. Here I was, writhing in agony and almost fainting on the grass due to the excruciating pain of a jammed finger. That's one way to mark the occasion!

For a couple of weeks, I sank. I started to get stressed. All the old fears tried to creep back on again. What if I had to go through this all over again? Then I remembered how faithful God had been in the past. He must want me to have this baby for a reason. It was His planning and His timing.

I decided I had only those two choices once again - stay like this, or fight and have the victory over my mind…and I knew the one I needed to follow. God seemed to say to me continually, "Just trust me with ALL your heart and DO NOT, repeat DO NOT, DO NOT, DO NOT lean on your own understanding (Proverbs 3:5-6). Stop trying to work it all out in your own mind. Stop even thinking about it. JUST TRUST ME!" It was a choice to trust Him, instead of everything else whirling around in my head.

I decided to take just one day at a time, absolutely refusing to think of the future. I had to be really strict with my thoughts. The enemy kept whispering his fear thoughts into my ears. Every time my mind would wander to tomorrow, or the birth, or post-birth, or next month or next week, I had to pull it back into line otherwise I would start to get all stressed. "Inch by inch, anything's a cinch. Yard by yard, it's too hard!"

It was during this time that I met the greatest counsellor in the world, the Holy Spirit! As I spent time with Him, My Personal Counsellor, I can truly say He is the best Counsellor you could ever get. He counselled me beautifully. I had no one to help me with this, but I just followed His lead. I knew I could trust Him to want only the best for me.

I had so much stuff that had been "stuffed" down on the inside of me. From the very time I was born, I had stuffed down the pain of parental control, manipulation, abuse and rejection. And this pain has to come up at some point. If it's not dealt with, it will come out in destructive ways such as depression, anxiety, anger or pain, or we can allow the Holy Spirit to take the lid off, in His timing, bringing up what He needs to and healing it in His time and power.

As I entered into this process with the greatest Counsellor in the whole world, I found the Holy Spirit didn't need to ask a whole lot of questions. As the All-knowing One, he instantly knew where the issue was and what needed healing, and He could go to that exact right spot. I was able to trust myself to His counsel completely. Over a number of months, he would bring up memories to me of traumatic childhood times in prayer.

Alone with Him, I would talk about them with Him and allow Him to take me back to revisit the feelings, thoughts and emotions of those times (in the Spirit). As I expressed what I had never been able to express before, sharing how it felt for me during those times, He brought me truth and perspective on them. I could then pray through each one under His leading, and then broke every fear, released forgiveness and allowed Him to minister healing to me.

Through this process, I was able to forgive my parents and receive a total release from all those terrible fears and trauma from the past. I chose to love my parents even though they did a terrible job at parenting. I released them to God. God is so good. He's the only one who can take away the pain and shame. I can honestly say there is no sting there anymore.

After my open and honest chats with Him, telling Him exactly how those times made me feel, I would curl up with Him (it was like pulling His Presence up over me like a blanket). Sometimes I would cry tears of grief and sorrow, but mostly they were gentle tears of healing. Tears of cleansing. The Holy Spirit knew exactly the right spot to touch, and He knew exactly what He was doing. "X" marks the spot, right deep down inside, right inside the deepest parts of my psyche and spirit. I would just let Him minister, and He was ever so powerful and ever so gentle.

I would sometimes picture myself curled up on my Daddy God's lap, and I would just ask Him to minister healing to me as I slept. It felt like the safest place in the whole universe! I didn't even need to know what He was doing or where He was healing. It just all seemed so complex and so deep.

Many times, I couldn't even put it into words how I was feeling. But He knew. And that is all that mattered. I told Him, "I trust You completely. Can you please minister to me while I sleep?" And I surrendered to Him fully. To this day, the Holy Spirit is still my greatest Personal Encourager, My Personal Coach, my called-alongside One, the Greatest Counsellor in the whole world. He is my closest and most intimate friend and guide. He counselled my heart back to wholeness and counselled me out of that dark place. He put the broken pieces back together.

The Holy Spirit healed me from flashbacks that haunted me at various times from my childhood, in particular with sexual abuse. Even though Ian and I had a healthy sex life from the day we married, I wasn't fully free because of the childhood trauma and abuse I had been subjected to. Those flashbacks and subconscious negative physical reactions kept haunting me.

After spending time with God, again, I had to start saying, "If Jesus has already set me free, past tense (free indeed), then I had better start acting like it, by faith". So I did. And He did. And the rest is history.

God can accomplish in a moment what would take years on our own.

I had an encounter with God one night by myself in my bed in our farmhouse, where the Holy Spirit came upon me, and I began speaking in tongues. I had been trying to express to the Lord how much I loved Him and how GRATEFUL I was to Him. I owed Him my life. How do I thank Him for restoring my mind to soundness, my emotions to peace and wholeness, and healing my exhausted body? Getting me back on an even keel? He literally saved me! He saved me from hell! The English language seemed so lacking to be able to express the depth of what I was feeling and wanting to pour out to Him. Somehow, "I love you Lord, I love you, oh how I love you so much! I can't express how much I love you with all my heart" over and over from the depths of my being just didn't do it justice, just couldn't express it fully.

Then suddenly it seemed like He appeared in my room, and I had an almost "out of body experience" where I was lifted up in the Spirit suspended, just me and Him. It was almost like He just lifted me out of all that "stuff".

*"He lifted me out of the slimy pit, out of the mud and mire;*
*He set my feet on a rock, and gave me a firm place to stand."*
*(Psalm 40:2 NIV)*

I now had the power of the Holy Spirit to overcome all those things I had struggled with before in my own strength. God had developed in me a strong faith, and I was so "sold out" for Him. I had a much deeper love for Him and a much greater desire to live wholeheartedly for Him than ever before. Jesus said of Mary: *"She who has been saved from much, loves much!"* (My take on Luke 7:47.) And that is truly my testimony.

I wouldn't have a life if it wasn't for Him, so therefore, my life is His. I wouldn't have it if it were not for Him. I honestly don't know where I would be. I am completely indebted, and I know that full well. I am completely grateful and am His forever. I have poured out my heart in gratitude many times, saying with heartfelt devotion: "I will go anywhere and do anything for you, Lord. Because I wouldn't have a life if it weren't for you."

My Redeemer lives! And that I know full well.

# CHAPTER 8
# NEGATIVE AND POSITIVE CONFESSIONS

My life motto is: "**Life is 10% of what happens to you and 90% of how you respond to it.**"

Why is it that some people have been through major traumas, and yet are the most positive, beautiful people you have ever met? And yet others get a tiny little pinprick from a rose thorn, and that is all you hear about! Because this is absolutely true - life is only 10% (a teeny 10%) of what happens to you and a whole 90% of how you respond to it.

As God started to heal me of the pain and memories of my childhood, I realized I needed to change my confession, what came out of my mouth. I realized that because of my negative upbringing, I had become a negative person, and you can never rise above the level of your confession. A negative confession is draining on your body. It is a vicious cycle. The more drained and tired you become, the more you speak negatively. But I discovered that if you give your body the right environment, with a positive, uplifting confession, it can actually heal itself.

Apparently, every seven years, each cell in your body renews itself. So, if you give it the right positive, optimistic environment, it will flourish. And add to that the Word of God, wow!

I continued to speak out positive confessions as my fourth pregnancy progressed. My favourite verse from the Bible is *"I can do all things through Christ who strengthens me,"* and it was a real lifesaver.

I couldn't believe how I flew through that pregnancy. I don't carry babies well, with terrible morning sickness for up to five months, plus a growing family (each of them prone to febrile convulsions, ear infections and tonsillitis). Through the winter months especially, I felt like I was always at the doctor with one of them. God gave me the victory. I clung to Him daily.

Every minute. I absolutely refused to let fear enter my thoughts. And oh, it tried. I clung to God's Word, I refused to let fear enter my thoughts, and I was really blooming by the time I gave birth to my fourth daughter.

It was my best labour and birth (although a breech birth). I had friends praying in tongues throughout the labour and birth. And what a blessing! She was adorable, with cute chubby rolls around her neck that I just wanted to kiss all the time. Four beautiful daughters! My heart was exploding toward God for His goodness!

Two weeks before our daughter was born, we joined a newly planted Spirit-filled church in our nearest town. I was so delighted when I heard the pastor speaking about this kind of outworking of faith – the things I'd had to learn the hard way.

At our country church, the minister would stand and explain away miracles, as if there was a natural explanation for them. I would come home feeling so deflated and worse than before I went to church, especially now that I knew how much power was in the Word of God. It was wonderful to hear faith preaching for a change! I praise God for the teaching and input these pastors had into our lives over the following five years.

We were so hungry for the things of God. So much so, that when our fourth daughter was only six weeks old, we enrolled for a Summer Soul School at our new-found movement's Bible College in Paraparaumu.

It was a week-long course with classes in the mornings and evenings, and we had the afternoons free with the family where we could go to the beach and explore the Wellington region. I still remember that everyone was incredulous that we had brought four children with us, one of them only a six-week-old baby who slept so beautifully in her pram. The course was about salvation and evangelism, and we gained such a passion for seeing people come to know Jesus Christ. It burned within us.

This expressing of positive confessions, when I was previously coming out of those darkest days, meant that when I came out in the morning and Ian would ask me how I was, instead of my usual answer of, "not doing very well", or "I feel terrible today," I would make myself respond matter-of-factly with "I believe I am healed." I certainly didn't feel like it, and I didn't want to pretend that I was good when I wasn't, but I had to make myself say it. And the more I did, the more I began to believe it!

This is faith, faith in the finished work of the cross. Faith in the Word of God. Faith in the power of God to heal; the very Word that proceeds from the mouth of God. I was already healed, I just had to walk in it, and call those things that were not, as though they were. I had to believe Him.

Saying, "I believe I am healed" is not lying. It is just saying what you believe. It is believing the Father's Word before you actually see it. If I was to say, "I am healed", or "I have been healed", all the while being fully aware that I haven't been, and obvious to others that I haven't been...that would be like lying. But to say, "I BELIEVE I am healed" is a completely different story. It's what I believe! Believing is not lying. I believe Jesus has done it for me; I believe He carried my sickness on the Cross; I believe that "by His stripes I am healed." Just like I believe that I am saved by repenting of my sins and confessing His Name as Lord. I am saved by faith! And what I believe will come to pass, so the Bible tells me.

This is a real discipline and involves surrendering to the Holy Spirit. I kid you not; it is the fight of faith! You're in a spiritual battle. The fight has been won by Jesus Christ, but your fight is to die to the flesh and to give in and live in the Spirit. I had to walk in the new creation that Jesus said I was, believing the old was gone and the new had come. I had to leave the old behind and put on the new. I had to believe, by faith, that I was free. I had to believe, by faith, that the old had been dealt with on the cross and was buried with Christ. I had to believe, by faith, that if Jesus said I was now free, then I had better start acting like it!

That meant in every area of my life that wasn't free, I had to start to declare that it was and begin to walk like it was free. That included how I saw myself - physically, sexually, emotionally, socially, relationally. It included my thinking, my confidence, my marriage, my parenting... every area was free in Jesus Christ! So I needed to start acting like it, otherwise I was making what Jesus did on the Cross of null effect.

To this day, after almost forty years of being a Christian, I still challenge my responses or thinking and ask, "Who told me that? And is it the truth?" That is the only way to keep dismantling the lies.

After we joined our new church, my husband also came into a total release in the Holy Spirit. One night, when our new pastor was praying over Ian to break the blockage that was preventing him being filled with the Holy Spirit, he turned to me and asked if there was any blockage in my life that could be hindering Ian.

No one was more surprised than me when under the anointing of the Holy Spirit, up from the depths of my being came the word "incest". I didn't even fully understand what that was and had never ever spoken it before to anyone. The shame and shock of it overwhelmed me, but we were both set free that night.

On Ian's part, he had held unforgiveness towards my dad and hadn't even realized it. It was like being born again, again. We just got even more "on fire" for God and never looked back

One of my initial greatest fears in my earliest days of recovery (as a still very new Christian) was that I was possessed, that I had demonic spirits inside of me causing me to be this way. Fearing that just made things worse because I was afraid of what they would do. The fear of that would paralyse me, and it took some undoing. It wasn't until I learned that the enemy has been defeated, disempowered and stripped of all his weapons that I realized he wasn't to be feared any more. Since Jesus came into my life, the devil had no power over me at all.

At the Name of Jesus, every demon must flee. Light and darkness can't dwell together. When the light came in, it would drive out the darkness. The only thing the devil had was his fiery darts, the lies that he would whisper in my ears all the time. He wasn't inside me; he was outside of me, just constantly whispering his lies in my ear.

Once I realized that, I knew all I had to do was to shut down those lies and not listen to them anymore. I became much more aware of those lies being whispered and shut them out instantly. I shut out all his negative putrid filthy lies and whispers of fear. I didn't have anyone pray over me and break off any strongholds over my life at that point. I had to suffocate them out and give them absolutely no room to breathe, filling my life and mind with the Word of God, so they eventually got tired and left. Satan's target is your mind, and his weapons are lies. So fill your mind with the word of God.

Years later, I remember hearing our lovely friend and evangelist, Trevor Yaxley, share about how he got woken up at night by a demonic presence at the end of his bed. He said, "Oh, it's just you!" then rolled over and went back to sleep because he knew the power of Jesus in and around his life! He wasn't going to be intimidated by some demonic spirit that had been defeated at the Cross. Smith Wigglesworth is quoted as doing something similar.

I never thought I'd say it, but I'm glad I went through these experiences. I haven't exaggerated any of these things; if anything, I've probably under-played them in trying to explain. I feel like I've had a taste of what hell is like in this battle of my mind and emotions. Torment of the mind has to be one of the worst agonies anybody can ever go through. But I am thankful because it has been through this battle that I have found places in God which I would never have otherwise. I continually praise God that He brought me through victoriously.

*"When I was at the end of my rope, He saved me."*
*(Psalm 116:6)*

*"I was right on the cliff edge, ready to fall, when God grabbed and held me...the hand of God has turned the tide."*
*(Psalm 118:13,16)*

*"There (I) called out to God in (my) desperate condition...*
*He got (me) out in the nick of time." (Psalm 107:6, 13,19,28 MB)*

*"What would have become of me, had I not believed that I would see the Lord's goodness in the land of the living!"*
*(Psalm 27:13)*

*"I didn't die. I lived! And now I'm telling the world what God did. God tested me, He pushed me hard, but He didn't hand me over to death."*
*(Psalm 118:17 MB)*

*"Oh blessed be God! He didn't go off and leave us.*
*He didn't abandon us defenseless."*
*(Psalm 124)*

*"Then the Lord said to Moses, '*
*Write about this battle in a book so people will remember.'"*
*(Exodus 17:13-15)*

# PART THREE
# NARCISSISTIC PARENTING AND ITS EFFECTS

# CHAPTER 9
# STRANGENESS AND ESTRANGEMENT – IT'S NOT JUST ME!

As THE YEARS went on, I started to realize that the way my mother had acted towards me was not just my fault, and not just towards me.

My mother was estranged from her brother and his family quite early in my life because she was jealous of her new sister-in-law. We didn't have relationship with those cousins because my mum loathed my aunty. At any family events, she would always be so critical of them and cause trouble against them, sometimes right in front of them or behind the scenes.

She also cut off my dad's only brother (and only sibling) and his wife because she thought they were "funny old things" and was so embarrassed at their quirky ways. I never knew until years later that they were actually lovely Pentecostal Christians, and the shame of that would have been why they were cut off. She was so vehemently against those "cranks" as she called them.

As I got older, she also cut off her only sister who was fifteen years younger than her. Again, through jealousy or perhaps some criticism of her. None of us had a clue why.

There were Irish relatives too, who regularly visited the family in New Zealand. My Pop came from a family of twelve, who were all still in Northern Ireland. When they visited, because of all the estrangements, they had to have separate gatherings with each faction of my family, mostly because they didn't like inviting my mum to anything.

In recent years, I have reconnected with all of these people including cousins. My aunties are lovely and not at all like they had been described. I have really good, loving relationships with them, and they have amazingly loving relationships with their own families, but they share so many stories of strife, deceit, manipulation, lies and constant enmity from my mother. They had no idea what was going on behind the scenes in our home. They would share stories of how everyone feared her, how she had to have the limelight and the attention, including how she would sit off in the corner of the room and judge everyone at family events.

There were stories told of how my mother would position herself or pose under a light (even in her later years), so that she would look her absolute best as if she was a movie star or beauty queen, and then pose there all evening, evaluating and looking everyone else up and down. I heard the nasty things she would say, including directly to my cousins about their appearance or life situations. The judgments and criticisms were foul. I have since heard about the manipulation and deceit that she was involved in regarding her own father's estate.

I share this, only to show that it wasn't just me experiencing or "imagining" these things and it helped hugely as it gave me some kind of closure that I wasn't the only one.

I have shared my testimony in different parts of the world over the past thirty-plus years, and mostly tried to downplay the control, manipulation and abuse from my mother partly because I didn't want to dishonour her or unwittingly make her the "scapegoat" for my life, or blame her for how I turned out, and partly because people may not have believed it could be so bad. I also wanted the focus to be on the transformational power of Jesus Christ working in one individual life to set them free.

However, when I came to understand both the term narcissism and what a narcissistic mother acts like towards her children and the effects it has, and all the lights came on. It was like a full-on revelation. Who knew there was such a thing? That was my story to a tee!

I felt like I was finally validated in thinking and feeling the things that I did, and it really WAS that bad, after all. You couldn't make this stuff up! Here it was in black and white, and I finally understood. This knowledge gave me a sense of validation and contributed to my journey of healing.

I had previously had people ask me if my mum was jealous of me, several times? I don't know what provoked those comments; they would never say.

Another sense of validation came when, while in Whakatane, we had a visit from my eldest brother and his (then) girlfriend. She was absolutely lovely but was having trouble trying to deal with all my brother's issues. As they were considering marriage, she had them both going to counselling together, and a lot of stuff was coming up.

The counsellor had suggested my brother talk about it to me to get my perspective on it and find out what more was really going on. My mother's actions had not only hugely affected me but also my brother.

I shared the huge things I had to overcome, and Ian and I both shared our testimony of what God had done in our lives. We really encouraged my brother to do the work necessary to get healed from his past. He seemed genuinely surprised that we were doing so well, enjoying ministry, and had a lovely home and family.

Unfortunately, his relationship with this lovely girl didn't make it, and he has continued to go through many relationships since.

Sadly, there were around 25 years of estrangement with my family, because of the rejection of our faith and strong disapproval of the steps we had taken to sell up everything to pursue ministry, and also because of the boundaries that I had put in place for myself and my family. Our last two Christmases with her, as a family, were full of silent treatment and disapproval, even after travelling three hours to be there. It was so awful, we didn't want to subject our girls to that any more (on Christmas Day of all days!) and so began our own family Christmases full of love, fun, laughter and celebration.

Her disapproval that I was now lovingly but firmly standing up for myself and couldn't be manipulated any more, meant we grew apart. All the years that we were estranged from my mother, I continued to reach out and honour her for the role she had in my life. I always sent her changes of address and phone as we moved around the country planting and pastoring churches. I sent her an annual Christmas letter with photos of the girls and letting her know our highlights and what we were getting up to. I let her know each time a grandchild was on the way, when each of them arrived, and sent her regular photos of each of them. I never heard back about any of them.

We invited them and each of my brothers and their wives to each of our girls' weddings. They did come, would sit together as a group, and she would do what she normally did, sit off to the side and look everyone up and down. It was always very strained, and the snide remarks kept coming. Occasionally, I would phone for one of their birthdays, and we attended the odd function like their fiftieth wedding anniversary party. It was always formal, cold and very brief.

The relationship always remained very much one-way. We would act like things were fine around them, pretending, but we really didn't feel any attachment to these people. All the interactions were so fake. We were an embarrassment to them because of the way we had chosen to live, helping other people, and the disapproval was long and strong.

There was one point, a few years into planting our first church in Whakatane when I received a call from my mother out of the blue. She wanted me to meet her at a neutral place, and I was NOT to bring Ian with me. That last point alone was enough to put the "wind up my sails". I really couldn't do it, and I didn't want to.

By now, I had some healthy boundaries around my life, and I didn't want to subject myself to any more abuse all over again. I agreed to meet her, but Ian wasn't going to let me go alone, and I was glad about that.

Imagine the anger when I arrived, and she saw Ian in the car. She was furious! It was pouring with rain, and we were parked down by the lake at Rotorua in a public carpark. She jumped in the back seat and demanded that I be in the back seat with her, without Ian. He wasn't going anywhere, especially not in the rain, thankfully for me. He stayed seated in the driver's seat and prayed quietly under his breath.

It all started again; the angry, accusatory tone, the put-downs, the belittling, the demands, the control and the manipulation. I hadn't encountered this for some time, and I knew that I probably wouldn't be able to say what I really wanted to say in her intimidating presence, so I had pre-written a letter.

I handed her the letter, briefly outlining the sexual abuse I had encountered as a child (not mentioning the abuse from herself). Some of those facts included, she wouldn't have known. The letter was written in love, but firm. I mentioned how I was very unhappy growing up and how those things had affected me greatly, but that I had found healing in Jesus Christ. I loved them as parents, and I had long ago released forgiveness and didn't hold anything against anyone.

Her angry response after reading the letter was, "How did I know that my own girls hadn't been sexually abused, or weren't being sexually abused right now?" That was all. There was no love, no acknowledgement, no reconciling with that spirit, and we ended up going our separate ways after being told in no uncertain terms that she was so disappointed and angry with me (and us both) that I hadn't come alone. She had her own agenda, and because Ian was there, she couldn't control me or try to overpower me.

"A controlling, dominating person
is not full of power but of fear."
(Danny Silk)

Even though I had prayed and asked the Holy Spirit to put a shield of protection around my heart, by the time we had driven an hour back to Whakatane and parked outside the school to pick up one of our girls, I shared with Ian that I felt the spirit of rejection trying to come on me all over again. He instantly prayed and broke that stronghold off my life, and I was able to put it behind and move on.

In her last few months of life, my mother called me from the Lion's

Cancer Lodge in Hamilton where she was staying. She said she had a growth on her lip that she was having treatment for, but that it wasn't cancer. She didn't want anyone to know that she had pancreatic cancer and was dying, as I found out later.

I received a call from a brother two weeks before she died, telling me if I wanted to see her, I should go now. Ian and I visited her at the hospice in Tauranga because she didn't want me to come to their home. It was very formal and awkward on their part, with small chit chat over a cup of tea. Ian and I responded with love and just treated them like we would have any other couple we were visiting pastorally, checking on how they were both doing. We left at the same time and went our separate ways. I reached out instinctively to give her a warm hug as I said goodbye (my family had never been huggers, but I certainly now was), and it was like hugging a rock. It was really strange knowing this would be the last time I saw her.

I still respected her as my mother and as a person, but there wasn't any emotional connection, apart from feeling sorry for her. Ian and I had both prayed beforehand and would have loved to have a meaningful conversation, or even talk about what she believed about life after death, but even though she was frail and wasting away, she was resolute and a closed book.

Even in death, appearances mattered to my mother. My dad later told me she had a full set of implant teeth screwed into her mouth so that she would look good in an open casket! She was terrified she might be seen without her false teeth.

Also, just before she died, she insisted that my dad sign the apartment they lived in over to her name. He had been diagnosed with a small cancerous growth also in her last few weeks, and she was so worried that he might die before her that she wanted the apartment in her name only.

After her death, my dad had to go to all the trouble and lengthy process of lawyer's fees to transfer it back into his own name. She seemed to only think of herself. She also had "their" only cat killed and placed in the casket with her! The cat would actually have been good company for my dad after her passing.

The funeral was so strained and difficult, with people from all different factions that didn't talk to each other coming together. My uncle, her estranged brother, had died just 24 hours before her, and we had just had his funeral which was a lot more light-hearted. But sadly, she had called him in his last few weeks of life and whatever she said to him, no one knows, he literally never spoke again. He was a closed book. He would just sit and stare out the window.

It was strange when the photos that came up on the screen at her funeral were mainly of her plants and her cat, and the most that was described about her was her gardening and her cooking.

She had planned the funeral, written the long eulogy about her life for the funeral director, and even laid out my father's suit and what he was to wear before she moved to the hospice to die. She had controlled right up to the very last detail. There was hardly a mention of family at all in her eulogy, but no one was more surprised than me when it was announced from the front, right in that moment, that I would be speaking along with my brothers.

I spent the whole time wracking my brain, trying to remember something positive to say about my childhood, and I felt so distraught that I couldn't remember anything but negative. Obviously, grief at the loss of my childhood and coming together as estranged siblings had a big part to play in that, too. In my heart, always wanting to honour, all I could do was thank her for bringing me into the world and honour her for giving me life.

Following my mother's death, I started to reconnect with my dad, and he always seemed happy to see us. I took him some meals for his freezer, as he didn't have a clue how to cook and look after himself, and after some time, he came to live with one of my brothers, just five minutes down the road from our house.

We visited him there a couple of times, celebrated his birthday and Father's Day with him and my brothers, and visited him in hospital after a major operation. He seemed like the same old dad we had always known.

My dad died within fifteen months of my mother, and I was glad I had a chance to reconnect over this time before his death.

## My God is my Heritage

Obviously, there were some good things in my childhood; many incidental details that would be impossible to share here. Unfortunately, they were usually overshadowed by my mother's ominous presence looming over us and controlling us at every turn.

We were financially well provided for, even though everything was meted out sparingly. I definitely wasn't an angel child, often getting involved in sibling rivalry with my annoying brothers as is normal in every home.

Our times at the beach during our teens contained some happier moments where we could get out of the house and away, going for long walks, long hours swimming and sunbathing, or climbing the mountain. My older brother and I would often go out for day fishing trips on a local charter boat.

However, I was definitely shaped by my upbringing in a negative way. It was only as I started learning more about narcissism and its incredibly damaging effects that I realized just how shaped I had been. I like to say shaped but not shattered! I owe this all to Jesus. Without Him, I don't know where I would be. My husband can vouch for the complete transformation Jesus has worked in my life.

I am so grateful that God gave me four beautiful daughters, and for the priceless relationships we all share. There's nothing like it. Each of them is so different... different personalities, passions and styles, but I cherish each one of them uniquely. And now I also have five beautiful granddaughters, along with four handsome grandsons.

A child deserves to be nurtured and loved. Children are precious, valuable gifts from God. We are just their caretakers for a while. They are not possessions, slaves or reflections of you. Their job is not to please you or make you happy. They belong to Him. We have this amazing privilege of pouring into them, building them up to really believe in themselves, to know who they are in God and to pursue everything they would love to do with their lives, making a huge difference in this world.

I guess all parents have the chance to take the best from each of their own childhoods and decide how best to replicate that in their own family, while also leaving the not so good things behind. There are no perfect parents, and we all make mistakes, but breaking the cycle means taking time to think about what kind of parent you want to be. I made sure to have a loving home, providing a safe place; fostering openness, closeness and trust with my children.

Ian and I identified the values that were important for us in our home and the kind of culture we wanted to build. We were determined to have a positive, uplifting home environment, a safe place where God is first. It gives us great delight to see our girls reproducing that in their own families.

I am thankful that I found the Lord and that it was He who conceived me and knew me even before the foundations of the world. It was He who knitted me together and ordained where and how I would be born. He uses parents to bring us into the world, and some of them don't do a very good job. But I came from Him. I was His idea, His offspring, His plan, His DNA.

This revelation helped me hugely in coming to terms with my identity, my heritage, my roots, and where I came from. In my mind and spirit, I was able to bypass my family heritage and realize that I came from Him. He was my roots!

Even though my childhood was incredibly difficult and damaging, I need to remember that I came from Him first and foremost. God wanted me and cherished me and looked upon His daughter with such passion and heartfelt love.

*"Even if my father and mother abandon (forsake, reject) me,*
*the Lord will hold me close."*
*(Psalm 27:10)*

# CHAPTER 10
# NARCISSISTIC PARENTING - WHO KNEW THERE WAS SUCH A THING?

Over the years, I have felt the judgment from many well-meaning Christians who tried to insist that I work to heal my relationship with my mother and tried to make me feel guilty for the ongoing estrangement. There was definitely an element of telling me that because I was a Christian, I should just get it sorted. They had no idea how much I tried. Without crawling back and putting myself back under that control and manipulation, there was no reconciling with her.

From what I understand now about "narcissistic parenting", I am incredibly grateful to God for allowing the separation, which allowed me to flourish into the real me, the whole me, and all He had destined me for. Not to mention saving our girls from the manipulation and control they could have come under. God knew with his impeccable counselling and His "All-Knowing-ness," which is far above what we can comprehend, what I needed.

It took me an awfully long time to speak about my testimony, mostly because of the guilt I felt at speaking against my mother. I felt like I was betraying her somehow, like I was that "naughty brat of a child" who was ungrateful, negative, and couldn't see any good or had imagined things. I felt like I was being dishonouring and betraying her, and deep down, I probably still excused her of a lot, preferring to own the blame myself. Because most girls really love their mums, right?

Sometimes I would catch glimpses of girls and young women standing with their arms around their mum having fun, or one of them leaning over the other seated, from behind, with their arms wrapped around their neck, just so natural and comfortable and happy in each other's presence. I never felt envious, but I used to wonder if they really realized how precious that was because I never had that kind of relationship. And I have compensated for that by trying to excuse her somehow, and taking a lot of the blame on myself, even though none of it was my fault.

Learning more about narcissism has helped me move forward in this. Some of the information below felt like it "read my mail". Finally, I understood what had been going on with my relationship with my mother and the way she acted towards me.

## What is narcissistic parenting/mothering?

Dove Christian Counselling describes it like this:

*"A narcissistic parent can be defined as someone who lives through, is possessive of, and/or engages in marginalizing competition with the offspring. Typically, the narcissistic parent perceives the independence of a child (including adult children) as a threat and coerces the offspring to exist in the parent's shadow, with unreasonable expectations. In a narcissistic parenting relationship, the child is rarely loved just for being herself or himself."*[1]

Psychologist Alice Marlowe says this (excerpts as follows):

> *"Narcissistic mothers control their children. They constantly blame others. These women are highly self-absorbed and have an over-inflated view of themselves. These mothers do not tolerate views that differ from their own and will not tolerate their children having views that do not align with their views. They are completely*

1 http://www.dovechristiancounseling.com/Narcissistic-Mothers.html

*oblivious to the needs of their children. Moreover, they are unaware of how their behaviours affect the psychological and emotional well-being of their children.*
*Children of narcissistic mothers are required to view the mother as she views herself, which is full of grandiosity and self-importance. Narcissistic mothers view their children as an extension of themselves rather than as separate, autonomous beings. Their children are expected to represent the mother as she views herself and wishes to be seen by the public at large. Narcissistic mothers use their children to fill their own emotional needs.*
*Mothers who are narcissists are intrusive and frequently ignore appropriate boundaries with their children. These mothers will cross emotional and physical boundaries with little regard to the child's wants or needs. At the same time, these mothers frequently neglect the basic emotional, and sometimes physical, needs of their children. Narcissistic mothers may use rage, physical abuse, blame, guilt and shame, criticism, and emotionally withdraw to control their children."*[2]

Lindsay Dodgson writes for INSIDER about Narcissistic parents, as follows:

*"Narcissistic parents create tension among all family members, and sometimes it's very covert tension, but it is at a chronic level. They will triangulate siblings, they spin stories, they tell half-truths, and you start to notice the pattern, just like in a romantic relationship, of how they create that chaos.*
*Narcissists try to pretend that they are perfect. They don't want to see any of their own flaws, and address the fact they are just normal, because in their mind they are superior."*[3]

2 https://wehavekids.com/parenting/The-Damage-a-Narcissistic-Mother-Does-to-a-Child-What-Stepmoms-Need-to-Know
3 https://www.insider.com/children-of-narcissistic-parents-are-either-favourite-or-scapegoat-2019-1

## How narcissistic mothering affects children

Joanna McClanahan, of Scary Mommy, writes:

*"Imagine growing up in a home where one of your parents couldn't truly love you. Where every time you looked to them for encouragement, you were told that you were stupid for even trying. A parent who viewed every act of independence as a threat and met each accomplishment in your life with jealousy instead of joy or praise. This is what it is like to live with a parent who is a narcissist. Recent studies confirm that narcissistic parents are incapable of truly loving others, even their own children.*

*Narcissists also view the world in a binary manner: Things are either viewed as special/ideal/perfect or worthless/harmful/garbage. There is no in-between, and they treat their children according to those extremes. This leaves their children wanting desperately to please them (to be on the "love" side of the spectrum, rather than the darker, more hateful side) and they'll even let their narcissistic parent control their lives, just to keep things running smoothly. Likewise, as long as kids cater to the narcissist's needs and make* them *feel good about themselves, they're more likely to respond positively, making the child's home life more harmonious. But as kids grow up, they become stronger, more confident, more brave. Narcissistic parents see their children's independence as a direct threat to the control they want or need over their lives.*

*Out of desperation to retain control, narcissists will try to deliberately sabotage their child's sense of self-worth. Some of the common tactics they use include creating unhealthy competitions, using guilt and blame, giving ultimatums, and/or putting their child down (by telling them they're fat, ugly, useless, stupid, etc.) to try to keep their child's confidence low.*

*It's not surprising that many kids who grow up in these types of unhealthy environments develop feelings of guilt and low self-esteem that they later carry into adulthood. Kids raised by narcissistic parents are less likely to develop a realistic self-image. It is brutal to grow up this way.*

*As children of narcissists become adults, they have to learn there's a difference between real love and narcissistic "love." And that includes coming to terms with the fact that what they've experienced is actually emotional abuse and constant gaslighting. After that, it's an uphill battle for children to accept that their parent's narcissistic actions aren't their fault or responsibility, as is true with any form of child abuse. If the relationship with their narcissistic parent is to continue, adult children of narcissists need to establish clear, firm boundaries — and stick to them.*

*Many adult children find that the most healthy option for them is to sever the relationship altogether. The cycle of abuse and control doesn't end because you've left the nest. Narcissists can't turn themselves off."*[4]

Lindsay Dodgson writes:

*"Narcissistic parents create a damaging environment for children to grow up in. Narcissistic parents are controlling and manipulative. If they have more than one child, they tend to pit them against each other. One child is usually the favoured child, while another is the scapegoat. Narcissists often emotionally reject a child that reminds them of their own insecurities and flaws.*

*As an adult, strong boundaries, detached contact, or no contact at all are the best ways to deal with the relationship."*[5]

More from Karyl McBride Ph.D, Psychology Today:

*So how does narcissistic parenting affect children? The child won't feel heard or seen. The child's feelings and reality will not be acknowledged. The child will be treated like an accessory to the parent, rather than a person. The child will be more valued for what they do (usually for the parent) than for who they are as a person.*

*The child will not learn to identify or trust their own feelings and*

4 https://www.scarymommy.com/narcissistic-parents-incapable-loving-children/
5 https://www.insider.com/children-of-narcissistic-parents-are-either-favourite-or-scapegoat-2019-1

*will grow up with crippling self-doubt. They will be taught that how they look is more important than how they feel. They will be fearful of being real and will instead be taught that image is more important than authenticity. The child will be taught to keep secrets to protect the parent and the family.*

*The child will not be encouraged to develop their own sense of self. They will feel emotionally empty and not nurtured. The child will learn not to trust others and will feel used and manipulated. The child will be there for the parent, rather than the other way around, as it should be.*

*The child's emotional development will be stunted. They will feel criticised and judged, rather than accepted and loved. The child will grow frustrated trying to seek love, approval, and attention to no avail. The child will grow up feeling "not good enough.*

*The child will not have a role model for healthy emotional connections and will not learn appropriate boundaries for relationships. They will not learn healthy self-care, but instead will be at risk of becoming co-dependent (taking care of others to the exclusion of taking care of self). The child will have difficulty with the necessary individuation from the parent as he or she grows older.*

*The child will be taught to seek external validation versus internal validation. They will get a mixed and crazy-making message of "do well to make me proud as an extension of the parent, but don't do too well and outshine me." The child, if outshining the parent, may experience jealousy from the parent. The child is not taught to give credit to self when deserved. They will ultimately suffer from some level of post-traumatic stress disorder, depression, and/or anxiety in adulthood.*

*The child will grow up believing he or she is unworthy and unlovable, because if my parent can't love me, who will? The child is often shamed and humiliated by a narcissistic parent and will grow up with poor self-esteem. They often will become either a high achiever or a self-saboteur, or both. The child will need trauma recovery and will have to re-parent themselves in adulthood.*

*Being raised by a narcissistic parent is emotionally and psychologically abusive and causes debilitating, long-lasting effects to children. It is often missed by professionals because narcissists can be charming in their presentation, displaying an image of how they wish to be seen. Behind closed doors, the children feel the suffocation of self and struggle with loneliness and pain. The narcissist is not accountable for their own mistakes or behaviour, so the child believes they are to blame and that they flunked childhood."*[6]

Julie L. H0all (Narcissistic Family Files), shares her experience as follows:

*"Having a relationship with a narcissist is incredibly difficult because they have little to no empathy for others. A narcissistic parent will walk all over their family — even their children — to get their needs met. Realizing and accepting that you have one or more narcissistic parents is a long and intensely painful road... because children, even adult children, continue to desire love and approval, often against all reason. Ultimately, asserting low or no contact with a narcissist parent can be a healthy, liberating choice. Creating distance with your parent means giving up the delusion that they will someday change and releasing the feeling of responsibility for them they may have instilled in you,"* [7]

I know that reading through this information will mean the lights will come on for many who read this book; who like me, never knew there was a name and description for the kind of behaviour they experienced from others.

With all my heart, I hope it brings validation and recognition for all you have been through and helps you on your path to healing. I would really encourage you to research more for yourself so you can find some meaning to your pain and give yourself permission to heal as well. There are more links and information available on my website.

---

6 https://www.psychologytoday.com/nz/blog/the-legacy-distorted-love/201802/the-real-effect-narcissistic-parenting-children
7 https://www.huffpost.com/entry/what-its-like-to-break-up-with-your-narcissistic-parent_n_5a1f1d16e4b037b8ea1f3f0f

# PART FOUR
# MOVING FORWARD

# CHAPTER 11
# GIVING YOURSELF PERMISSION TO HEAL

## Normal Reactions to Abnormal Life Experiences

Dr Caroline Leaf says:

*"Depression, anxiety, PTSD… these are all normal reactions to life and being human. We have to change the narrative around mental health and stop looking at it as simply a chemical imbalance (which has been disproven by numerous scientists and studies) or a broken brain problem. How can we say, for example, that a mother who just lost her child and is depressed from the grief is depressed because she has a chemical imbalance? Also, simply focusing on the biological causes for mental health (which do exist but are not the ONLY causes) and ignoring the social and psychological only results in us looking at very few solutions and takes away from each and every person's story and history. Mental ill health has many causes and many solutions. What I want you to take away from all this is that if you are going through a tough mental health time right now, it's not because you are "broken" or due to some "chemical imbalance" in your brain. It's because life is hard, and*

> *sometimes really bad things happen or maybe you are in a work or family environment that is not healthy. But just know that these periods are not permanent, and your situation can change. Choose to listen to the depression and see what it's telling you - what needs to change in your life? What is going on deeper inside of you? Be honest with yourself even though it's scary. 'Depression is a normal response to abnormal life experiences" (Allen Barbour)."*[8]

I felt extremely guilty, the very first time I told my story to someone or shared it as a testimony amongst a group of women. I felt like I was betraying my parents and would get into trouble for it. I also carried extreme guilt and shame – making it difficult to admit that I had some previous mental ill health. I felt like it would lead to people judging me or treating me differently or assuming I was weak.

As I was raised with the feeling that I was bad and that my parents' unhappiness was my fault, I had to work very hard to change those thoughts. I was used to believing negative things about myself. Even when people would give me compliments, I found it very hard to receive them.

There must have been some good times in my childhood, and I often wrack my brain to try and remember them as I feel guilty for not remembering more. My mother's coldness, control and manipulation and the emotional, physical and sexual abuse **overshadowed everything** on a subconscious level. At such a young age, we form opinions about ourselves and what happens in our families. Because of how we were treated, we can easily jump to the conclusion that may or may not be true - the common belief - "I am not good enough."

I was stuck with the same thoughts about myself and others in my life - a negative cycle. This is why it is so vital to learn to challenge these thoughts and see things in a much more positive way. Now, I understand that these thoughts and feelings are completely normal for any

8 Dr Caroline Leaf (PhD, BSc) is a cognitive neuroscientist, and a skilled minister on mental, physical and spiritual health. You will not go wrong with any of her books or products.

survivor of childhood abuse. Part of healing is to stop pretending and covering up that secret which was buried in denial.

When children are raised on a diet of criticism, judgment, abuse and loathing, it's only a matter of time before they take over from those parents, delivering with full force to themselves the toxic lashings that have been delivered to them.

## Toxic Parents

Toxic parents come in many shapes. Some are so obvious that they can be spotted from space through the eye of a needle. Some are a bit more subtle. All are destructive.

A toxic parent has a long list of weapons, but all come under the banner of neglect, or emotional, verbal or physical abuse. Toxic parents lie, manipulate, ignore, judge, abuse, shame, humiliate and criticise. Nothing is ever good enough. A toxic parent treats their child/children in such a way as to make those children doubt their importance, their worth, and that they are deserving of love, approval and validation.

The truth is that you, like every other small person on the planet, deserved love, warmth, and to know how important you were. You're not useless at life – you've bought into the messages that were delivered by a parent too broken to realize what they were doing. But it doesn't have to stay that way. It is possible to heal from toxic parenting. It begins with the decision that the legacy of shame and hurt left behind by a toxic parent won't be the way your story will end.

The following are some excerpts from Geanne Meta's newly released book (shared with permission), which I have had the privilege of previewing and reviewing before her launch in August 2019 - "Parenting Well After Childhood Abuse - Be a great parent even if yours were crap."[9]

I highly recommend this book if you are coming out of a childhood abuse situation.

9 Meta, G. (2019). *Parenting well after childhood abuse: Be a great parent even if yours were crap.* Florida: Independent.

Geanne states:

- Once things come up from your childhood, it's important not to bury them or let them go back into hiding. The main thing to realize is that you weren't responsible for anything that happened. You were supposed to be protected and nurtured.
- Maybe your parents did the best they could with what they were given. They may have just been continuing the cycle of what was done to them. However, that is NOT an excuse for mistreating their children.
- Break the cycle of blaming yourself. Challenge how you think about yourself and what happened to you. You probably learned to deny and downplay the actions of your abuser. It may take some work to really understand that whatever treatment you got as a child was NOT YOUR FAULT. You deserved to be taken care of and loved.
- You're not obligated to take care of people's feelings who didn't take care of yours.
- Once you remove the veil of secrecy and allow yourself to accept the reality of what happened, it will get better. Give yourself the gift of calling yourself a survivor. You may have been a victim when you were young, but you had an inner strength that helped you survive. Give yourself credit for all that you've overcome and believe that you can handle whatever comes next.
- Boundaries were a foreign concept to me because my feelings and needs were over-run as a child. My body was not my own. I had no voice to say "No". I was taken advantage of and didn't have any rights. I learned the necessity of setting boundaries for my kids, though. I wanted them to know about respecting boundaries and how to set them.
- Home was an insane situation that had nothing to do with how lovable, good or bad I was. It took a long while to learn to love and respect myself.
- When you remember yourself as a child and realize your

innocence, you can begin to break the cycle of shame and self-blame. You can learn to give love to yourself.

- You must become emotionally healthy to meet the challenges of parenting. That includes getting out of denial. You must learn healthier ways to treat yourself and find the courage to heal. You can learn to break free of the dysfunctional ways your family of origin operated in. Change your negative self-talk, or you will most certainly pass it on to your children.
- Not everyone can handle hearing about incest and child abuse. They may not know what to say, and you can end up feeling more isolated. Talking about child abuse is uncomfortable. Most people are just not equipped to be helpful and may respond in ways that are hurtful without intending to. Even best friends may not respond well because they just don't know what to say.
- Geanne recommends a wonderful book, "You Can Help"[10] by Rebecca Street, an abuse survivor, as a guide for loved ones.

## The way out is by faith!

If you ever find yourself hemmed in with thoughts and beliefs about yourself that are weighing you down, causing you to feel trapped and in the pit, I want to encourage you that broken things can become blessed things. Once you've examined your life and confessed all known sin, and there is no demonic influence in that area, that is, you've rebuked the lies of the enemy and had ministry in that area (strongholds broken), the only way out is… BY FAITH!!!

Can I encourage you to access all the ministry and counselling you can. But once you have done this, you need to walk out that ministry and knowledge by faith. Some people feel that they need to keep going back and back for counselling, but the fact is, there comes a point where you have to stand in faith!!

Don't stay in bondage to emotional turmoil from past lovers, failed relationships, broken family cycles, or old ways of thinking. Broken things CAN become blessed things… it's time to receive your healing.

10 Street, R. (2016). *You can help: A guide for family and friends of survivors of sexual abuse and assault.* New York: Createspace.

# CHAPTER 12
# TURN YOUR SCARS INTO STARS!

The last few decades of my life have been busier, more pressurised and demanding than ever before, but also the most fulfilling. From a timid, shy, nervous person who would never have a go at anything, God has totally transformed my life. I've shared some things in my story that I wouldn't normally (they don't have a hold over me anymore) only to show what Jesus can do with your life if you allow Him to. IF YOU ALLOW HIM TO!

I've found myself doing all sorts of things I would never have thought I could. Instead of staying locked into that old thinking and saying, "What? I can't do that! I've never done that! I'll just watch you do it," now I will have a go at most things. Ask my husband and he will tell you, I'm a lot more adventurous now! I'll venture out of my comfort zone, and I've done all sorts of things in the strength of the Lord.

My motto, **"I can do all things through Christ who strengthens me"** has been key. Just the mere fact that I am writing this book is testimony to the transforming power of Christ. Just the sheer number of messages I have preached in New Zealand and in various other places around the world, sometimes in large conferences, is testimony to the transforming power of Christ because I used to be so self-conscious, so painfully shy and tongue-tied. I didn't like the spotlight on me and shudder to think of how insecure and painfully awkward I was around crowds. I would freeze, go bright red and cry when the pressure of people looking at me and the pressure to speak overwhelmed me, so I avoided it at any cost.

People look at pastors and leaders and their wives and think, "They've got it all together. Probably always have had. They don't understand me or where I'm at." Wrong! I want to tell you that we're human, just like the rest of you. We're forgiven sinners, too. God takes us through things that we might better understand and better minister with compassion. That's the only way any of us grow, as we allow Him to change us and use us for His Kingdom. That's how we **turn our scars into stars**!

I'll have a go at just about anything now. I've found myself knocking on strangers' doors and speaking to people about Jesus Christ. At Bible College, I found myself preaching and song leading – a real first for me back then. Instead of saying no, I did it! The Lord and I did it together.

In Whakatane, where we planted our first church, I regularly put myself out there with the rest of our enthusiastic crew and did street preaching. From witnessing with a street church team in the red light district of Kings Cross in Sydney at night; with ambulance sirens blaring around us, fights, stabbings, drunks falling out of the bars and lying at our feet with their bottles... to Tel Aviv, Israel, putting myself out there to do street evangelism with our crew from Jaffa and NZ, bowling up to complete strangers of all different ethnicities and interacting with them about the gospel.

I have sat with newly saved members of Black Power or Mongrel Mob gangs in their homes, discipling them in the foundations of the Word and teaching them God's plan for marriage, while at the same time I'm just as happy sitting with millionaires in their homes discipling them in the foundations of God's Word.

We have planted four churches and watched God making something out of nothing. It is always such a delight to see Him do that!!

In discussing our marriage on our 43rd wedding anniversary

this year, we both agreed that one word describes it best - full of ADVENTURE!

We were two quiet, shy young people who walked out of that church 43 years ago, and now we have embarked on so many adventures, pushed the boat out, taken faith leaps beyond our years, challenged status quo, found ourselves doing things we never dreamed possible, challenged our thinking, pushed ourselves to the limit and out of our comfort zones so many times over the years. No ordinary life, that's for sure.

From successful farmers and raising a family of four daughters, to selling up everything to go to Bible College, and subsequently church planting, God has been with us. We've had 22 house shifts, overseas adventures, and wonderful times hot air ballooning, fishing, boating, water-skiing, horse-riding, mountain-climbing, tenting, caravanning, motorbike riding, cycling, and lots of hilarity and pranks. We've been involved in children and youth leadership, church leadership, conference speaking, pioneering new territories and ministries, radical evangelism, crazy miracles, hundreds of people reached for Christ and lives radically changed (I could write a book on that one right there), cross-cultural living and experiences, four faith kids, nine grandchildren, four crazy son-in-laws (Maori, South African, Australian-born and German), stretching ourselves financially, living by faith, raising other radical leaders including our four daughters, living an open-hearted, limit-busting, open-handed generous life way bigger than ourselves because we have a BIG God… and so much more it is impossible to include it here.

There have been so many times over the years we have been pushing the limits and living on the edge, and I have found myself starting to feel stressed or wanting to freak out, and my husband has reached out to squeeze my hand and say, "Just see it as an adventure, hon."

When you take the brakes off and go with it, you learn to relax and just enjoy the crazy, wild ride. Here we are 43 years later, still embarking on new adventures, building a new house, pursuing new dreams and pushing new boundaries. As Ian says, we have grown through it all; we've laughed and cried and everything in between.

Have I still got scared and wanted to chicken out over the years? For sure. All the time. But when I know it is what God wants, and not just me, the Holy Spirit and I have had such fun pushing the boundaries, smashing those fear barriers and doing impossible things together on mission. I have learnt to just "lean into Him" and let Him lead. He has brought out the best in me, and we have lived such an adventure-filled life.

Ian and I sold up our prospering dairy farm plus stock and machinery and everything we owned in answer to the call of God on our lives, moving on into full-time ministry. Launching out in faith and trusting God to provide for us was not an easy thing after always having the security of a farm and a secure income behind us. A large income!

When we decided to do that, my parents and brothers made it clear they were against it. The communications and disapproval became so difficult that we eventually drifted apart. My mother would always cut people off emotionally if she didn't approve of what they were doing. The only way you could ever get back into her "good books" was by crawling back, apologising, bowing and scraping and agreeing with her way of thinking. Even then, you would be made to pay and grovel.

I had plenty of experience of that over the years, but in this case, having grown stronger, I wasn't going to be emotionally manipulated by that anymore. I felt that loss, though. It was 25 years of estrangement, without any family because my brothers went along with what she told them and also cut contact. But in other ways, the severing of that awful control, once and for all was something that I needed. You can forgive someone and yet give yourself the respect of not being damaged by them any further.

We set values for our own family, to build the kind of culture we wanted our girls to grow up in. These values came out of our strongest and deepest convictions in God. Culture can happen by default or by design. We knew the kind of family environment we wanted to create. We probably didn't always get it right, nobody does, but we worked hard to give our girls the most uplifting, faith-filled, positive, big-thinking, empowering life that anyone could have. We are so proud of who they are, and the difference they are making in so many lives around them. They are all faith girls and such influencers!

After moving off our farm into town to work with our local church, I felt the Holy Spirit say, "Don't get too comfortable, because you're not staying here." Within six months, we had given up our mortgage-free dream home and left dear, special brothers and sisters in the Lord as we moved away from our beautiful home church, moving on in our call to serve the Lord. First in Rotorua and then in the Eastern Bay of Plenty.

It seemed to me at times that the Lord was removing all my props, so I had to rely solely on Him. That's not bad for a person who used to be so insecure and full of fears of the unknown. Again, the things I had learned through those tough days of my journey to recovery held me in good stead and provided the keys I needed to keep breaking the boundaries.

When we arrived in Whakatane, we didn't know a soul. We had only the Lord, each other, and the vision He had placed in our hearts; a passion for people to know Christ and a deep assurance and faith in Him. It wasn't long before we had two beautiful churches (in Whakatane and Opotiki) that grew quickly with lots of new people being saved on a weekly basis, and we knew heaps of people!

We have countless stories of outreaches on maraes, in halls, schools and theatres where so many people came to know Jesus Christ from all different walks of life, eventually buying a pub and transforming it into a vibrant church centre to develop and train all these new believers into leaders and influencers. This hub became a spiritual home overflowing with youth who were looking for hope and purpose in life, so many lives changed and impacted for eternity. One of those is our son-in-law, who is now pastoring with our daughter.

"God pulled you out of the pit so you could reach back in and get more people out… NEVER forget that."

After eight years, we moved to our nation's biggest city, Auckland, to plant a new church on the North Shore, and again saw so many people from all different ethnicities come to Christ. I still remember how huge and daunting Auckland appeared when we first moved there, the huge skyscrapers, the millions of cars, all the billions of lights as far as the eye could see at night just blew my mind. The thought of ever driving in Auckland was daunting, but again, I started one block at a time.

Once again, God made something beautiful out of nothing, and we grew a flourishing church there. It is not something we ever take for granted because many new church plants don't get off the ground. Our young leadership team was involved in planting a second service at Massey University to reach even more people for Christ. Again, our outreaches were large and varied, drawing people from right across Auckland city. Our vibrant youth ministry saw so many youth and young adults coming to Christ and training in leadership.

Twelve years later, after leaving this church in the hands of capable pastors developed under our leadership (another daughter and son-in-law), we moved two hours south to Hamilton, where we took over an established church back in the region where we both grew up and set about to reach a new community for Christ. Again, we have seen God do amazing things, growing a thriving and healthy church in a new housing area.

At numerous times throughout these 30 years of ministry, I have found myself speaking at churches, conferences, camps or meetings throughout New Zealand, in London and Australia sometimes as the sole or keynote speaker. That was not me; it had to be God! Was I freaking out beforehand? Did I want to chicken out? Absolutely! Especially when speaking in front of other well-known pastors and world-class speakers. But I continued to step out in faith, completely dependent on the Holy Spirit growing, stretching and anointing me and guiding me in what to say. I could have easily said, "No, that's not me. I could never do that!" It is faith all the way. I know countless speakers who will tell you the same... we're actually all chickens on the inside. And if you could do it on your own, it's probably not God, anyway.

The unique stresses and demands for anyone working in the people field are well-documented, with many burning out. People can be so difficult to deal with at times, and the pressures can be great, that if you didn't know who you are in God, you wouldn't last. Add to that the normal pressures of raising a flourishing family in the ways of God (and watching out for the individual members of your family with each of their unique needs) plus making sure you don't neglect your own wellbeing or your marriage...the demands are huge. Life can bring huge financial pressures at times, packed schedules, huge expectations, and sometimes even betrayal of dear friends or colleagues; sometimes the pain of life is so great that it takes everything you have to get back up again.

There have been major dramas we have had to face, including my husband being beaten up by someone who came for counselling. And yet, God's calling and empowering has been more than enough. I am so grateful for His anointing and constant presence journeying with us. We have never wanted to take this awesome privilege lightly and have needed Him every step of the way.

In the midst of it all, our beautiful eldest daughter was diagnosed with a cancerous tumour wrapped around her spine at the age of 21 years. The outlook wasn't good, with a high possibility she would end up in a wheelchair. Watching her strong faith for healing, but then end up having to go through a long and delicate surgery and the intense and ongoing pain she has had to endure then and since, including the possibility of not being able to have children, have all been absolutely massive. The stress of that is huge for her as well as her parents. To see her strong faith, and miracle after miracle is priceless. Despite the odds, she walked out of that hospital.

A few months later, her dad was able to walk her down the aisle to be married to the love of her life. She has two very handsome and sporty sons who are absolute miracles, but that is another story. These days she lives a very full and productive life as a pastor, reaching people for Christ and seeing them discipled in the ways of God. She has such grit and resilience developed through those times.

To walk with two daughters through their long and painful roller-coaster of infertility has also been a massive journey for us all. Through that journey, thankfully, bladder cancer was discovered and stopped in the tracks for one of them. To see the miracles God has worked through it all is mind-blowing. We have nine beautiful grandchildren to prove it; every one of them a miracle!

What I am trying to show you is, I have been through far more stress and pressure in subsequent years, huge disappointments and heart-breaking situations that could have broken me or wiped me out, and yet the things I learned through those critical years of recovery have been hugely helpful, and I am eternally grateful that I have not ever had a recurrence of that debilitating fear, depression, panic or anxiety attacks. God has given me real courage – where before there was no backbone at all. He has built this resilience and bounce-back ability. He has set me free in so many areas of my life, and I've been able to minister to so many others as a result.

After 30 years of age, I was finally free to be me. Free to be what He made me to be, free to love my children and grandchildren, free to be a great mother and wife. Free to be adventurous and to enjoy life. Free to love and enjoy people without fear of hurt or rejection. Free to try new things, step out in faith and walk on water. Free to serve God and love those He brings across our path. That's my testimony of God's power to transform!

## Being transformed

The Bible says, *"Do not conform to the pattern of this world, but be transformed by the renewing of your mind" (Romans 12:2).* The Greek word for "transformed" used here is "metamorphoo". When we are born again, we are new creatures; we have metamorphized – changed. The Bible tells us Jesus has done a complete and total work. He doesn't do things by halves. "It is finished". Complete! Whole! Total! The old has gone, the new has come. In Christ, you are not just a better version of your old self. You have been made new.

The only trouble is, after a while, we start to slip back into some of our old thought patterns. We're still thinking like the old person, instead of the new one. Old warning lights come on – be afraid! You can't cope! You're not good enough!

To be transformed by renewing our minds is a continuing work. To let the Holy Spirit reprogram us to bring about this renewing of our mind will transform the rest of us! Disciplining our thought life means watching what you put in, and the people you spend time with. Our past life doesn't need to hold us back. It need not be a hitching post to keep us tied up, but a signpost for the future. All that negative conditioning in the past can be reprogrammed by the Holy Spirit working in our lives.

We're all born into that negative tendency (that old sin nature) because Adam sinned, remember? But we've got to want to break out – be set free – and enter into all that Jesus Christ has done for us. There is no point in holding onto it and saying, "Well that's just me, just the way I am – you don't know all the things I've been through – they did this to me – and she did that to me – and he said that – that's why I'm like this."

"Saying, 'This is just who I am' will cause you to never take accountability for your behaviour and will cause you to NEVER CHANGE." (Matt Sorger)

In studying and reading about the great healing evangelists, revivalists and reformers, many of them came from lowly backgrounds, and God called them as children. Many of them overcame huge, insurmountable problems, including severe health issues and handicaps. God taught them to die to those things and to themselves. Who said YOU couldn't do it?

Not long before we moved to Whakatane to plant our first church, we were in Australia at a conference. We were privileged to hear Dr Larry Lea speak. He wrote the popular book, "Could you not tarry one hour?" about prayer. That man was saved in a mental hospital by reading Matthew 4, 5, and 6, and then led his friend to the Lord using the same chapters.

When he was released from the mental hospital, he went out on the street and preached, and he had 1000 youth respond to his first altar call. He led them to the Lord by (you guessed it) reading Matthew 4, 5 and 6.

Only five years later, that man had a church of 10,000 people in a town of 7500 people (Church on the Rock, Rockwall, Texas with 48 pastors). I've never heard such a powerful preacher. He was a quiet, unassuming, humble man, but the anointing just dripped from him. As he walked down the aisle at one stage, everyone felt the tangible presence of God coming near.

His associate pastor was his friend who he led to the Lord in the mental hospital. At the same conference, we heard a lady speak who was saved as a schizophrenic. She heard God tell her she was going to be an "evangelist" and became one of the most sought-after women speakers in Australia. That's God's transforming power! The power to set us free. And God can use anybody.

I am so grateful to God that He has set me free. I know what it's like to be saved from much, so I love Him much (Luke 7:36-50). I truly believe you can walk this journey to freedom as well.

# CHAPTER 13
# FREE TO BE ME

As I HAVE travelled and ministered in churches, conferences and different groups around the world, I'm amazed at the number of women (some of them even in their 50's and 60's) who have been abused as a child, sexually. So much sexual abuse is heart-breaking, and so many have fought with depression, fear and/or anxiety for years or other mental health issues for years. Many have been on anti-depressants for ten years and longer, and it breaks my heart.

After I have spoken, many come up to me, sometimes tentatively and privately, to tell me that as they listened to my story, it was a replica of theirs, and they were crying out to be set free. They have been through so much, but they hope now, to escape.

I have sat and counselled with dear, precious women, with very little self-worth and no sense of identity, who decades later are still trying to break free from their controlling mothers or the effects of them. Still, the greatest joy of my heart is to see the transforming work of the Holy Spirit and the Word of God go to work in precious hearts and lives, and to witness the amazing results.

Christ came to set the captives free. FREE!!! John 8:36 says, "If the Son sets you free, you will be free indeed." Can you honestly say you feel free? Free to leave the past behind. Don't let it rob you of the joy of living today.

Jesus said, "The Spirit of the Lord is on me because He has anointed me to preach good news to the poor. He has sent me to proclaim freedom for the prisoners and recovery of sight for the blind, to release the oppressed, to proclaim the year of the Lord's favour." That's you! And that's what the Christian life is all about; setting people free and seeing them released into their fullest potential in God. Free to be yourself – who God created you to be – beautiful on the inside, beautiful on the outside. When you're free, there is a beautiful glow about you as you are absolutely filled with the glory and fullness of God.

This kind of freedom for the captives of abuse has been the cry of my heart for years. There are so many people taken captive by the enemy who need to be set free. The stories are the same all over the world. And Christ has anointed each one of us to carry on that work - to see people released from bondage and come into the fullness of Jesus Christ.

*"The thief comes only to steal, kill and destroy.*
*Jesus has come that they may have life and have it to the full."*
*(John 10:10)*

When you're free in God, you are free to be the woman (or man) of God He has created you to be:

- You are free to launch out in faith and trust Him completely in His perfect plan and purpose for your life.
- You are free to be used by Him in ministering to the captives and seeing them set totally free.
- You are free to be the wife and mother He has created you to be, or the single woman sold out for Him that He has created you to be.
- You are free to develop new talents, abilities and giftings that you didn't even know you had.
- You are free to live adventurously with the Spirit, going all out for all that God has got for you.

- You are free to be carried away on the wings of the Spirit into new heights in God.
- You are free to be you! Uniquely you, beautifully you, passionately you; perfect, complete and satisfying to your Father in heaven.
- Free to love the Lord your God with ALL your heart, with ALL your soul, with ALL your mind, and with ALL your strength!
- Free to love and to be loved.
- Free to have fun and enjoy life.

Free in every way. No longer bound by fears and insecurities but full of faith! It's a delightful place to be – no masks, no skeletons in the closet, totally transparent and clean. If nothing else, I would exhort you to go for all that God has got for you. Don't settle for second best; go for God's best! Don't shrink your theology down to the level of your experience – but please, please, please dare to lift your experience up to the level of true theology.

Don't let the enemy have the last laugh. Jesus defeated him at the Cross. Take great pleasure in rising up and reminding the enemy that he no longer has any power over you to hold you trapped with these things of the past. You're a winner, not a loser. Every one of you is a powerhouse of potential, just waiting to be released. Only the Holy Spirit can do that, as YOU – and only YOU – allow Him to.

Ian and I could still be back on the farm, doing our own thing, if we hadn't been open to God taking us on as far as He wanted to. I'm not saying that everyone has got to give up their jobs or business, but we all need to be prepared to let God take us as far as He wants to – not placing any limits on Him and what He can do in our lives. That's being free!

Don't stay locked into your past but allow the Lord to gently peel away those things that have "crusted" over you. He wants to reveal that beautiful, special and unique shining personality that is inside, bursting to get out.

Paul says in Phil. 3:13, "One thing I do, forgetting those things which are behind and reaching forward to those things which are ahead, I press toward the goal to win the prize for which God has called me heavenwards in Christ Jesus."

God says – the Bible says – You're a child of God! You're a daughter/son of the King! Reach out and allow that to be real and true in your experience today. Don't sell yourself short – let the real you stand up and come out! The Christian life is exciting, fulfilling, challenging. Don't hold back and only experience a little of what God has for you. Put yourself back on that Potter's wheel today and let Him mould and shape you into that beautiful vessel.

We can only be truly free in Jesus. There is NO other Name. It saddens me greatly that people are not prepared to mine the depths of Him and find themselves set free in the process. They would rather take the easy option and continue to stay in their issues and insecurities, often going from human to human looking for help, or continually talking about their problems, instead of fully going to the only ONE who has all the answers: **Jesus + Nothing = Everything!**

Paul writes, *"If any man is in Christ, he is a new creation" (2 Cor. 5:17).* That one Scripture alone will revolutionise your life if you speak it out and meditate on it, letting it become living in you. You're not just a forgiven sinner – not a poor, weak, staggering, sinning church member. You are a new creation created in Christ Jesus with the life of God, the nature of God, and the power of God in you! Satan's dominion has been broken. He lost his dominion over your life the moment you became a new creation. Disease and sickness can no longer lord it over you. The old habits can no longer lord it over you. God is in you now. You face life fearlessly – you know now that greater is He that is in you than all the forces that can be arrayed against you.

The Word of God is alive and active, and faith works. I am a living testimony of it. If He can make something out of my mess, He certainly can with yours! But to be that woman or man of God – who has a bold confession of who she is in God – you need to know God's Word. Get into it – eat it – drink it – sleep it. Believe it! Live it out in your life! That will be what will change you.

It starts with a decision – a choice YOU make! We can hitch our life to our past hurts and failures and stay there – or we can use them as a signpost to the future. Are yours a hitching post or a signpost? To help you, I would love to send you "Who I am in Christ – what God's Word says" - please feel free to email me using the contact details at the back of this book, or download from my website.

When you meet Jesus face to face, and He looks in your eyes – just Him and you – you might be still full of excuses and looking for sympathy. And it would be heart-breaking to have Him look you in the eye and say to you – "Are you saying that My agonising death on the Cross, all the pain I went through for you, was not enough? That My blood was not good enough? That My power was not sufficient for your weakness? That it wasn't worth it? I paid the ultimate sacrifice, but it wasn't good enough?"

It's time to go in and possess your own personal promised land, instead of continually coming to the Cross in shame and struggle. It is time to possess all that's rightfully ours! Don't just settle for the status quo. Break out of average and mediocrity. If we're going to be history-makers, we've got to go in and take our rightful inheritance – our promised land. Or we'll be like the Israelites, walking around and around in the desert. They never even got to see what the promised land looked like, they were so wrapped up in self and unbelief and negativity.

Instead, when I come face to face with Jesus, I want to be like it is mentioned in Rev. 3:17. The Bible says He will give us a white stone with a new name written on it. C.S. Lewis puts it something like this – When He looks into our eyes, that new name, known only to He and us, will be like a symbol of all that we've been through together. There will be an exchange in that glance. An understanding. He gets it! Where we've allowed Him to turn our scars into stars! They've become jewels in our crown! And we've become better people because of them – not bitter!

As I conclude, I want to remind you of the four key lifechanging decisions and choices I made to bring me out of the rut:

1. Am I going to stay this way for the rest of my life? I have two choices:

    a. To lie down and accept it and live a life of hell, or
    b. To stand up and fight my way out, with the Lord's help (take full responsibility, stop blaming or using excuses).

2. Decide if God's Word is truth or not, and then if I believe it is true, act like it.
3. Get rid of "stinking thinking" and "slack speech".
4. Go in and possess all that God has for me.

What old mindsets do you need to get rid of? It's time to start believing the Word again – not just for your church or for your city – but for your own life! Will you make a commitment, if God shows you an old mindset, to get rid of it? Or will you cling to it, and make excuses for it because it is far more comfortable? It's time to be free; free to be you, free to be me!

**IT TAKES GUTS TO LEAVE THE RUTS! I DARE YOU!**

# PART FIVE
# FAITH BITES

In the final section of this book, I want to share some quick and very practical tools that can help you leave the ruts. If you are anything like I was, you are just desperate for someone to give you some keys to help you get out of this place. You're crying out, "Can someone please help!" These are keys that worked for me and that you can begin putting into practice **straight away**. They will give you hope and provide sure stepping stones that will help you walk your way out.

I have called them "FAITH BITES" on purpose, so you can take one bite at a time, and not feel like you have to digest them all at once. They are in no particular order, and as there are over thirty of them, you could use them as a devotional or morsel to chew on and to work on every day for a month (repeating over and over again as long as you need to). You will find your faith begin to grow the more you put them into practice.

I found it helpful to summarise the key points on a card and keep in my pocket or somewhere handy so, when I was going through a rough time, I could remind myself the things to focus on doing. You may also find this helpful because in this initial state, where your mind is all over the place and you can't remember what to do in the moment, it gives you something to focus on and put into practice. Strangely, that in itself can help to calm you and gives you back some control.

Some people think faith is believing for something, but we've got to WALK BY FAITH, not by sight or by feelings. It's time we got real and start appropriating the Cross. To me, it's simple. If God says it – I believe it – that settles it. If He says I am a new creation, then I am. The reason so many of us are weak Christians, even though we are sincere and earnest, is that we have never dared to make a confession of what we are in Christ or who we are in Christ. Our very lives are denying the power of the Cross! These tools will help you find out who you are in the mind of the Father, how He looks upon you, and begin to speak in line with that.

A lifechanging motto I learned from Dr Robert Schuller is this: *"The Me I see is the Me I'll be!"* If you see yourself as weak, shy, timid, insipid – then that's how you will be. But if you see yourself as a beautiful, confident, funny, friendly, happy child of the living God – then that's how you'll be.

Your faith will never grow beyond the confession of your mouth. God's Word is alive and active – it is living, it's pumping, it does things! God created the world through WORDS! His word can also create and recreate in us. I encourage you to use these faith bites to help you appropriate and work out these truths. Be blessed.

# KEY 1

## "LIFE IS ONLY 10% OF WHAT HAPPENS TO YOU, AND 90% OF HOW YOU RESPOND TO IT."

ALTHOUGH WE DO not always have the power to change every unpleasant circumstance in our lives, we do have the power to change our outlook. We can look at life from our innermost being, with our hearts filled with positive thoughts and attitudes, or we can respond, allowing the events of life to shape our thoughts and attitudes. This is a decision that only we can make – no one else can make it for us.

*"Some people could be given an entire field of roses*
*and only see the thorns in it.*
*Others could be given a single weed*
*and only see the wildflower in it.*
*Perception is a key component to gratitude.*
*And gratitude a key component to joy."*
*(Amy Weatherly)*

*"What we see depends mainly on what we look for."*
*(John Lubbock)*

Sadly, we can waste most of life with the misconception that joy and enjoyment come from our circumstances, but the truth is that they come from our ATTITUDE toward each circumstance, rather than from the circumstance itself. Obviously, nobody enjoys a troubling or painful circumstance, but if we look at it in a hopeful, faith-filled way, we can watch God work all things out for our good (Romans 8:28).

Enjoying life begins with the thoughts you choose to think. Yes, it is that simple! No matter what is going on in your life today, if you will choose happy, hope-filled thoughts, you will FEEL happier. Our thoughts are intricately connected to our feelings, so if we want to feel better, we need to think better. We cannot catch good thinking, but we can choose it.

We will need to choose good, positive, and godly thoughts on purpose and every day that we live. I don't think they will ever come so automatically that we never have to put forth an effort.

The way to put off your old life and put on the new, enjoyable life that God offers us is by renewing our minds and attitude daily (see Ephesians 4:22-24).

No matter what happened in your life prior to you being able to make your own choices, the fact is that if you make good choices, the results of those choices will ultimately overturn anything bad that has taken place before. There are countless testimonies from people who endured horrendous circumstances early in life, but through a strong faith in God, good choices, and hard work have now turned their lives around for the greater good.

An unhealed person can find offense in pretty much anything someone does.

A healed person understands that the actions of others have absolutely nothing to do with them. Each day you get to decide which one you will be.

Viktor Frankl, an Austrian neurologist and psychologist and Holocaust survivor, who suffered the atrocities of Auschwitz Concentration Camp, says:

> *"Everything can be taken from a man but one thing: the last of the human freedoms - to choose one's attitude in any given set of circumstances, to choose one's own way." (Victor Frankl)*

Charles Swindoll (a well-known Baptist preacher and author) says:

> *"Words can never adequately convey, the incredible impact of*

*our attitude toward life. The longer I live, the more convinced I become, that life is 10% what happens to us, and 90% how we respond to it. I believe the single most significant decision I can make, on a day-to-day basis, is my choice of attitude. It is more important than my past, my education, my bank account, my successes or failures, fame or pain, what other people think of me or say about me, my circumstances, or my position. Attitude is that 'single string' that keeps me going or cripples my progress. It alone fuels my fire or assaults my hope. When my attitudes are right, there's no barrier too high, no valley too deep. No dream too extreme, no challenge too great for me." (Charles Swindoll)*

William James, the father of American psychiatry, has said that:

*"The greatest discovery of my generation is that a man can change his destiny by changing his attitude of mind."*
*"We can alter our lives by altering our attitudes."*
*(William James)*

Attitude is a mindset! It is the way you look at things mentally. Your attitude is never static. It is a continual process. It has been observed that successful, mentally healthy people, regardless of age or profession, are not automatically positive. These individuals continually search for ways to maintain and improve their positive attitude.

- No one can have a positive attitude all the time.
- Excessive optimism is not realistic.
- There are times when we do feel down, but winners are those who can regain their positive attitudes quickly.
- When someone jars your mental focus into a negative direction, those who are positive, know that in order to bounce back, adjustments must be made.
- A positive attitude is the outward manifestation of a mind that dwells primarily on positive matters.
- Attitude is truly an inside job!

A Quote from Dr Billy Graham:

*"The happiness which brings enduring worth to life is not the superficial happiness that is dependent on circumstances. It is the happiness and contentment that fills the soul even in the midst of the most distressing circumstances and the most bitter environment. It is the kind of happiness that grins when things go wrong and smiles through the tears. The happiness for which our souls ache is one undisturbed by success or failure, one which will root deeply inside us and give inward relaxation, peace, and contentment, no matter what the surface problems may be. That kind of happiness stands in need of no outward stimulus." (Dr Billy Graham)*

Some people endure horrendous loss and traumatic circumstances in their lives, yet they have the most positive attitudes and amazing hearts of gratitude. And yet others experience a tiny prick from a rose thorn, or a tiny offense, and that is all you hear about…their life is ruined. Why? Because …… **"Life is only 10% of what happens to you, and 90% of how you respond to it." You choose.**

**When you can't control what's happening, challenge yourself to control the way you respond to what's happening. That's where the power is.**

# KEY 2
# IS GOD'S WORD TRUTH OR NOT?

If God didn't keep His Word and perform it in your life – He would be a liar! You can stake your life on God's Word because it is the TRUTH! The first thing every Christian must fully realize is that the Holy Bible is truly the **inspired and infallible Word of God.**

**All of the Bible** has been given to us by "**inspiration of God**" through holy men who were "**moved by the Holy Spirit**" to write what they wrote! All of the words in the Bible have come directly to us from God the Father through the Holy Spirit. The specific authors of the Bible then wrote under the guidance, inspiration, and illumination of the Holy Spirit.

This is why you can completely trust that what you will read from the Bible will be 100% pure, solid, God-truth! There is no other book on our earth that contains **direct words** from God the Father and His Son Jesus Christ. God Himself has arranged that all of the revelation He wants us to have in this life about Himself, His Son Jesus, and His Holy Spirit would all be contained in this one incredible Book.

> *"**All Scripture is given by inspiration of God**, and is profitable for doctrine, for reproof, for correction, for instruction in righteousness, that the man of God may be complete, thoroughly equipped for every good work." (2 Timothy 3:16)*
>
> *"... knowing this first, that no prophecy of Scripture is of any private interpretation, for prophecy never came by the will of man, but **holy men of God spoke as they were moved by the Holy Spirit.**" (2 Peter 1:20)*

If God is all-perfect and all-powerful, then this means His intelligence and knowledge on all things is all-perfect. And if His knowledge on all things is all-perfect, then this means that all the words He is conveying to us in the Bible can be counted on as being perfect words, thereby giving us perfect knowledge.

> *"**Every word of God is pure;** He is a shield to those who put their trust in Him. Do not add to His words, lest He reprove you, and you be found a liar." (Proverbs 30:5)*
> *"**The words of the Lord are pure words,** like silver tried in a furnace of earth, purified seven times." (Psalm 12:6)*

Theologically speaking, the Bible is God's inspired revelation to man - from beginning to end. It not only contains the written Word of God; it **is** the Word of God - alive, active and **the truth**! (Hebrews 4:12) The very words spoken from God's own mouth. It is "God-breathed".

- **Plenary inspiration** = (plenary means "full")
    - All scripture is God-breathed, not merely some parts.
- **Verbal inspiration**
    - Every word is God-inspired, not just the ideas.

The Bible carries with it the divine authority of God. Not only is Scripture inspired and authoritative, but it is also inerrant and infallible. Behind the word of God, is the very throne of God, all that is Truth. The very integrity of God is woven into the pattern of His Word! You've got to settle that in your heart once and for all. Otherwise, you're double-minded and confused and won't receive anything from the Lord (James 1:8).

Often, we think we believe, but it is not until we have to depend on it for dear life that we find out if we REALLY BELIEVE or not. The bottom line is, if you want the divine truths that are contained in the Bible to really be able to change and transform you – then you will have to believe that all of the Bible comes directly to us from God the

Father through the Holy Spirit. If you do not, then the Bible will have little or no transforming effect on you and your life.

The truth found in the Word of God is more reliable and trustworthy than our fickle emotions and feelings. God's truth is unchanging, and that's why it is a solid foundation for us to stand upon. Unlike our emotions, God's truth will never let us down or lead us in the wrong direction. Reminding ourselves regularly that **"truth trumps feelings"** is a way of prompting ourselves to set the Word of God as our standard of truth and fix our eyes and hearts upon it daily.

When I was struggling with anxiety and depression, I threw myself on the Word of God like I never had before, saying, "God, if your Word is truth, and I believe it is, then prove it!" People sometimes say, "I've tried that, and it didn't work for me." Trying it is not enough! You've got to live it like your life depended on it! Knowledge is not enough; you've got to have faith in it!!

God's Word is a SOLID ROCK you can stand and depend on, and it will not let you slip. It will transform your life. No one can tell me otherwise, now. In the simplest of terms, *"faith is belief plus trust. It is resting in the person of God and His Word to us"* (Kent Hughes).

Faith is an active practice built on belief. It is not ambiguous; it's not unsure. It's a concrete conviction. It's the present-day confidence of a future reality. Faith is solid, unshakeable confidence in God built upon the assurance that He is faithful to His promises. Faith says that what God has promised will happen, and it's so certain that it's as if it has already happened. Faith treats things that are hoped for as a reality.

Faith has to have a foundation, and it is the Word of God!

# 🔍 KEY 3
## "GOD'S WORD IS LIVING AND ACTIVE - IT WORKS!"

The Word of God is at work within you:

> *"Indeed, the word of God is living and active, sharper than any two-edged sword, piercing until it divides soul from spirit, joints from marrow; it is able to judge the thoughts and attitudes of the heart." (Hebrews 4:12)*
> *"The word that God speaks is alive and full of power (making it active, operative, energising and effective." (Hebrews 4:12 AMP)*

The words in the Bible have God's **supernatural power and life** in them. They are anointed by the power of the Holy Spirit Himself. This is why the words and truths contained in the Bible have the supernatural ability to change and transform you into the kind of person that God wants you to become in Him. The Word of God is powerful; it is undefeatable.

*"Is not my Word like fire, declares the Lord, and like a hammer that breaks the rock into pieces?"*
*(Jeremiah 23:29)*

God's Word has God's power and His energy. The Bible says that the Word of God does not return void; it does His work, powerfully so (Isaiah 55). When it is declared in faith, it produces life. God's Word is not a word which is spoken and then drops to the ground and turns to dust. It is not like a dead leaf; it is like a living plant. It will accomplish what He desires and achieve the purpose for which He sent it.

*"Not one word of all the good promises that the Lord has made to the house of Israel had failed; all came to pass."*
*(Joshua 21:45 ESV)*

*"So shall my word be that goes forth out of my mouth; it shall not return unto me void, but it shall accomplish that which I please, and it shall prosper in the thing for which I sent it."*
*(Isaiah 55:11)*

*"And Samuel grew and the Lord was with him, and He let none of His words fail (to be fulfilled) or fall to the ground."*
*(1 Samuel 3:19)*

*"It is the Spirit who gives life; the flesh profits nothing. The words that I speak to you are spirit, and they are life"*
*(John 6:63)*

*"This is my comfort in my affliction, for Your word has given me life."*
*(Psalm 119:50)*

*"Your words were found, and I ate them, and Your word was to me the joy and rejoicing of my heart …"*
*(Jeremiah 15:16)*

*"How sweet are Your words to my taste, sweeter than honey to my mouth!"*
*(Psalm 119:103)*

The Spoken Word of God is powerful! It defeats the enemy. It is a cleansing agent. It is creating a powerful spiritual world around your life. It shifts, changes and rearranges things. It lifts and edifies. It brings comfort and hope. It shields, nourishes, produces fruit and smashes through barriers. It increases faith and brings victory, plus so much more.

As you are speaking and affirming God's healing and powerful Word over your life, you can know and picture that it is living - it does stuff - it has all authority - it is actively working in and around your life, creating, healing, setting free, restoring and breaking yokes, accomplishing what He says it will. You can trust His Word implicitly. His Word is truth and has all the authority and power of heaven backed up behind it. It works!

The words of the Bible are anointed by the Holy Spirit Himself – and they have the full ability to completely change and transform you, if you are willing to work with the divine truths that are contained in the actual words.

Jesus says in the Bible that you shall know the truth and the truth shall make you free. However, you first have to know what the real truth is before the truth can start to work to set you free.

# KEY 4
## "WORDS CREATE WORLDS"

God's words are omnipotent (all-powerful). I love how the Bible explains that "God spoke" and the worlds came into being. He is an expert at creating something out of nothing - "ex nihilo" - nothing, zilch, nada, zero, not a single thing, nought, void. God simply spoke, and the entire universe sprang into being!

He can create something out of nothing in your life too. Because we have been created in God's image, our words are potent, no matter how we use them, for positive or for negative.

Words create worlds - either a godly world or a demonic world over and around our lives.

- Faith and unbelief are built out of affirmations.
- The affirmation of a doubt – builds unbelief and fear.
- The affirmation of faith – builds strength to believe more.

To affirm is "to assert strongly, declare, confirm, pronounce, agree to, proclaim, profess, state explicitly, make known, avow, swear, certify, make a statement of fact."

**The truth is, we will never rise above the level of our confession.**

If you have ever read any of Frank Peretti's Christian novels on spiritual warfare, you will know that he describes how we can invoke a demonic presence (or world) around our lives, just by the words we speak. Our words are powerful. They are creating either a demonic world around our lives or a godly world full of His presence.

**"Flies don't hang out around an area where it is disinfected."**

Many of us are affirming lies over our lives every day and these lies are keeping us in bondage - lies of unbelief, fear, failure and unworthiness. You need to do a check-up on the words you are affirming over your life.

**"You won't get to the palace talking like a peasant."**

*"I tell you the truth, if anyone says to this mountain, Go throw yourself into the sea, and does not doubt in his heart but believes that what he says will happen, it will be done for him. Therefore, I tell you, whatever you ask for in prayer, believe that you have received it, and it will be yours." (Mark 11:23)*

***"You may have a heart full of faith, but is your mouth saying it?"***

Our words make us or break us! When I was in a very fragile state, one word or thought could send me spiralling downwards. That's how powerful they are. I realized after a while that I was a very negative person. When I came under pressure, what was in my heart came out. All negative words and thoughts that didn't line up with the word of God.

We need to train our mouths to speak in line with our new nature – God's nature. We need a check-up from the neck up!

Sometimes, when I didn't know what to think or feel, I would just start walking up and down in my room declaring what I knew to be truth from God's Word: "I believe you are Jesus, the Son of God. I believe You are who You say You are. I believe you died on the Cross for my sins and were buried in the grave. On the third day, you rose again, setting me free from the power of sin and death. I believe that You are seated at the right hand of the Father. Your Name is the name that is above every other Name…"

Within moments, I would feel full of faith. Something had shifted in the spiritual atmosphere. The enemy hates it when you speak out truth, so do it as much as you can!

God desires not only that His children believe truth, but also that we speak it. *"I believed, therefore, I have spoken" (2 Cor. 4:13).* God ordains that words of faith have more power than thoughts of faith alone: *"Say to this mountain, "Move from here to there" (Matt. 17:20).*

We need to function in the full throttle of power that God desires to give us. His desire is for us to use our mouths powerfully for His Glory. There is power in the words we speak. Build yourself up by quoting the Word of God and speaking in your heavenly language. When you speak in your heavenly language, the Holy Spirit is praying perfect prayers through you.

If you would like more information or help in speaking out God's word, I have made "Faith Confession" sheets and will gladly send them to you if you email me using the contact details at the back of this book.

# KEY 5
## "THE ME I SEE IS THE ME I'LL BE"

You couldn't be more righteous today if you tried! (Ephesians 2:6; Col. 3:1) This is an amazing truth that will change your life. You have got to start seeing yourself as God sees you. If you see yourself as a filthy rotten sinner - that is who you will be. If you see yourself as a lowly, timid, shy, hopelessly inept person - that is who you will be. If you see yourself as constantly failing, defeated, rejected, damaged goods, useless, never measuring up, and that people don't like you - that is who you will come across as.

BUT…if you see yourself as the amazing child of God you are and believe He thinks the sun shines out of you - that is who you will be. You will put your shoulders back, hold your head up and walk in that confidence. If you see yourself as kind, generous, loving, open-hearted, caring - that is who you will be. If you see yourself as confident and loved in Him, set free and with the Holy Spirit shining through you -that is who you will be. If you see yourself as cleansed, washed whiter than snow, made righteous and seated in heavenly places with Christ Jesus - then that is who you will be.

I am convinced that most Christians see themselves struggling from the bottom up. What do I mean by that? They see themselves as sinners, working hard to become a better person and to overcome their sinfulness, often beating themselves up and often failing. In actual fact, the Bible tells us we are already spiritually seated in heavenly places with Christ; blood-bought, cleansed, made righteous! You couldn't be any more righteous!

If we saw ourselves as that, we would be that! Seeing ourselves as made righteous and pure before God causes us to live and act like that. It causes us to walk in power and from a place of victory. Again, it's a faith thing. It's already done.

Are you building your life around what is wrong with you, or what is right about God? Many people spend their whole lives trying to 'get their life right.' What people really need is the revelation that Jesus has already made it right. If you are trying to live right, you will end up in condemnation, anxiety and depression, and ultimately, you will fail. Why? Because you cannot live right. The key is to live out of the rightness of God. Everything about Him is right; He can do no wrong. When you live out of Him, you live out of a position of victory, hope and blessing. You live out of who God is rather than out of who you are. As you understand and apply the righteousness of God in your life, it will cause you to flourish.

The enemy (devil) will always focus on everything you have done wrong. Your response is to focus on everything Christ has done right! So many of our mindsets are wrong when it comes to the Lord. We have to allow the Holy Spirit to strip away all those old mindsets of misinformation and mistaken beliefs and replace them with the truth!

If you have a poor self-image, as I did (understatement), I recommend you read the story of Mephibosheth in 2 Samuel 9. It will help you see not only why you are living far below the level God intends for you now, but also why you are in danger of missing out on what He has in mind for you in the future.

David said, *"Is there still anyone left of the house of Saul to whom I may show kindness for Jonathan's sake?"* (2 Sam. 9:1) David had a desire to bless someone in Saul's family for Jonathan's sake. One of his servants reported that Mephibosheth was alive and living in a town called Lo-debar. (Lo-debar means "pastureless," probably a place of poverty.)

Why would a king's grandson be living in such a place? Why hadn't he come to the palace, claiming his rights and privileges as the son of Jonathan, who had covenant relationship with the present king? He surely understood covenant relationship - everyone did in those days – and that it extended to children and heirs.

In ancient Israel, when two people entered into a covenant relationship, everything each of them possessed was made available to the other. It also meant that they would help one another, fight for one another, and do anything necessary to meet each other's needs. Yet Mephibosheth, the rightful heir of Jonathan, King David's covenant partner, was living in poverty. Why?

When news had come to the palace that Saul and Jonathan had been killed in battle, Mephibosheth was just a child. Hearing the dreadful news, his nurse ran from the palace with him in her arms - and during her escape, Mephibosheth fell and was crippled in his legs as a result (2 Sam. 4:4).

When David sent for Mephibosheth, he fell before the king and displayed fear. David told him not to fear - that he intended to show him kindness. Mephibosheth's response is an important example of the kind of poor self-image we all need to overcome.

David said to him - *"Fear not, for I will surely show you kindness for Jonathan your father's sake and will restore to you all the land of Saul your father (grandfather), and you shall eat at my table always."*

And the cripple bowed himself and said, "*What is your servant, that you should look upon such a* ***dead dog*** *as I am?" (2 Sam. 9:6-8)*

Mephibosheth had such a poor self-image, a **dead dog** image, that instead of seeing himself as the rightful heir to his father's and grandfather's legacy, he saw himself as someone who would be rejected - otherwise he would have already gone to the palace long ago to claim his inheritance.

A poor self-image causes us to operate in fear instead of faith. We look at what is wrong with us instead of what is right with Jesus. He has taken our wrongness and given us His righteousness - and we need to walk in the reality of that truth. That dead dog image will hinder us from being all we can be and having all we can have in life.

David blessed Mephibosheth - He gave him servants, and land and provided for all his needs: *"So Mephibosheth dwelt in Jerusalem, for he ate continually at the king's table, even though he was lame in both feet." (2 Sam. 9:13)*

This story was me to a tee, and I relate Mephibosheth's lameness to our own weaknesses. Yes, we have faults and weaknesses, but we may still fellowship and eat with our King Jesus. We still have a covenant with God, sealed and ratified in the blood of Jesus Christ. We offer God what we have, and He gives us what He has. He takes all of our sins, faults, weaknesses and failures and gives us **His** ability, **His** righteousness, and **His** strength. He takes our poverty and gives us **His** riches. He takes our diseases and sicknesses and gives us **His** healing and health. He takes our messed-up, failure-filled past, and gives us the hope of a bright future.

He loves to make something out of nothing!!

It's almost like we're watching Channel 1 and the best, most amazing movie is on Channel 3 - but we just didn't know. We didn't know what we're missing out on! We're tuned into the wrong channel, where the devil would love us to stay.

So how do you see yourself? Because - **"The Me I See is the Me I'll Be!"**

# KEY 6
## "POSSESSION THEOLOGY VS REDEMPTION THEOLOGY!"

I WANT TO TEACH you about a revelation that changed not only our ministry but our lives. Many of us are still living in 'Redemption Theology'. God has brought us out of Egypt, and we're saved by the power of the Cross – but we're still camped at the Cross. We are still struggling with sin and low self-worth, and life is hard every single day. Many times, we are confessing the same sins over and over again.

But God has a Canaan, a Promised Land, for each of us to Cross over and go in and possess – to go on in and take that land flowing with milk and honey that He has secured for us – that GOOD land – with huge grapes and pomegranates and a rich inheritance – that He said He HAS ALREADY given us - it's already ours! We just have to step up and go in and receive it by faith!

It should have taken the Israelites only eleven days to travel through the wilderness and into their Promised Land. But with all their negativity and murmurings against God, their hankering after the past, their focusing on the giants and their grasshopper mentality, they kept on going around and around the wilderness for 40 years. Some of us can be like that!

The incredible thing is that God had already told them that He had given them the land:

*"See,* ***I have given you this land.*** *Go in and take possession of the land the Lord swore he would give to your fathers..."*
*(Deut. 1:8)*

*"For the Lord your God* ***is bringing you into*** *a good land of flowing streams and pools of water, with fountains and springs that gush out in the valleys and hills."*
*(Deut.8:7 NLT)*

*"When you have eaten and are satisfied, praise the Lord your God for the good land* ***He has given you.****"*
*(Deut. 8:10 NIV)*

We must leave Redemption Theology (saved but still begging at the Cross) and catch hold of Possession Theology. Redemption Theology is awesome... we must always keep the Cross in sight, but we don't stay there. God bringing the Israelites out of Egypt, out of captivity, "Crossing them over" and leading them into their Promised Land is a typology of our salvation. So many Christians have still yet to get hold of that. This promised land is available to us now – here on earth – not just when we get to heaven! That's what faith is!!

God's unconditional love has brought us out of Egypt and set us free from bondage. Now we're free to go in and take possession (by faith) of all that's rightfully ours – all that the devil has stolen (and he will have to give back double for your trouble).

It saddens me greatly that much of the church is still coming from the bottom of the heap, TRYING to be good enough, TRYING to live a good Christian life, but feeling like they are never making it. That is what sin is – "missing the mark". A lot of messages preached in church are from that angle, telling us how much we are missing the mark, instead of telling us who we ALREADY ARE in Christ!

A powerful key in parenting is that your children will become who you tell them they are. If you speak over them all their failings, that is who they will become. Conversely, if you speak over them constantly who they are in Christ, how God sees them, that is who they will become. It is the same principle in our adult lives.

Salvation is not just a one-time thing - it is a continuous present tense. The diagram below illustrates:

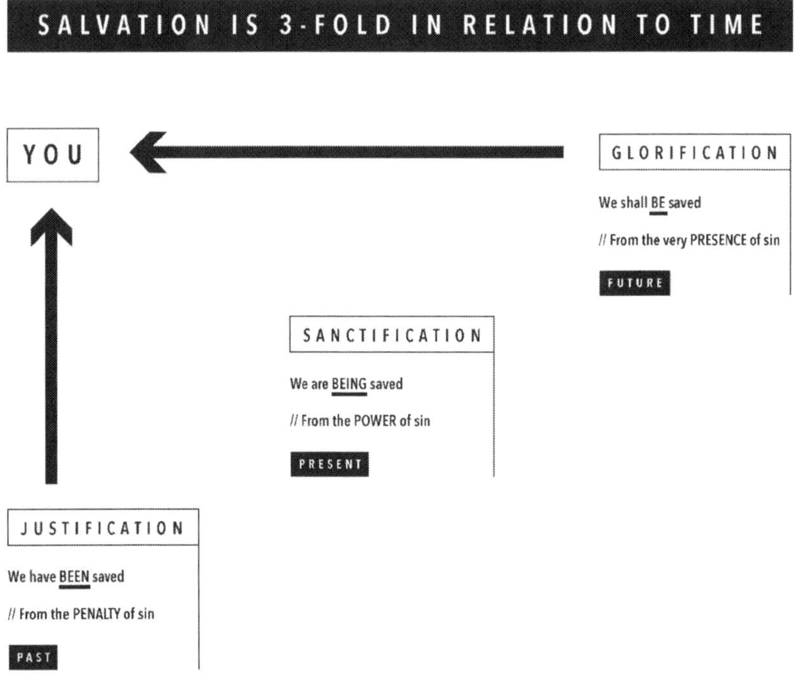


Right now, God sees you as already glorified, seated at the right hand of the Father with Jesus in the heavenly realms. Yes, in the natural realm, we are still here on earth, we are fully justified (just as if we had never sinned), still growing and "working out our salvation with fear and trembling" and still being sanctified on our way to heaven. But in the spirit, we are already made righteous. Glorified. That is how God sees us.

God is not linear and locked into time like we are. He is the great I AM; He sees everything all at once. In theology, they describe it like this: "He has simultaneous possession of His total duration." Think about it like this - instead of time being a line (how we see), it is more like a circle, where God is up above seeing everything all at once. **In His eyes, He already sees you as made righteous. You couldn't be more righteous today if you tried! That is truth!**

*"And God raised us up with Christ and seated us with Him in the heavenly realms in Christ Jesus."*
*(Ephesians 2:6)*

*"Since then, you have been raised with Christ, set your hearts on things above, where Christ is, seated at the right hand of God."*
*(Colossians 3:1)*

We have got to start seeing ourselves as God sees us! It's so simple – it is already done – we just have to receive and walk it out it by faith!

Have you ever thought how sad it would be to be living on a goldmine and never know it?

*The great-grandparents of a friend of Benny Hinn's went from a struggling existence in Kentucky to Oklahoma because they heard that it was the land of opportunity. The land they farmed on wasn't very productive and consequently, they never had much to live on. They eked out an existence. Eventually, they sold the land and moved to another state.*

*The person who bought the land from them discovered oil and became wealthy. The reason the land wasn't very good for farming was because it was so saturated with petroleum nothing would grow. Think of it! For years, these dear people lived near poverty when at their very feet was all they needed, not only to survive - but to thrive! If they had dug a little deeper in the ground, a gusher would have come up!*

*In the same way, we have the great resources of the Holy Spirit at our disposal, and yet some of us live our lives in spiritual poverty and frustration, not using the riches that are at our immediate beck and call.*

As the old saying goes, "You can lead a horse to water, but you can't make it drink!"

We ARE sitting on this goldmine that is ours, yet so many of us are not going on in and possessing all that is rightfully ours. Why? Perhaps because of ignorance (not knowing, incorrect theology), or perhaps because it does take some extra effort to really live by faith – it is a fight. Even though God had given the Israelites the land ALREADY, they still had to go in and fight some battles to occupy the territory that was rightfully theirs. A lot of Christians are just not prepared to do that.

I pray that just the fact that you are reading this book shows that you are one of those who wants to receive all God has for you and are not prepared to settle for staying where you are at.

*The story is told of a young man who was ready to graduate from college. For many months, he had admired a beautiful sports car in a dealer's showroom, and knowing his father could well afford it, he told him that was all he wanted. As Graduation Day approached, the young man awaited signs that his father had purchased the car. Finally, on the morning of his graduation, his father called him into his private study. His father told him how proud he was to have such a fine son and told him how much he loved him. He handed his son a beautifully wrapped gift box. Curious and somewhat disappointed, the young man opened the box and found a leather-bound Bible with the young man's name embossed in gold. Angry, he rose his voice to his father and said, 'With all your money, you give me a Bible?' and he stormed out of the house.*
*Many years passed, and the young man was very successful in business. He had a beautiful home and a wonderful family but realized his father was very old and thought perhaps he should go to him. He had not seen him since that Graduation Day. Before he could make arrangements, he received a telegram telling him his father had passed away and willed all his possessions to his son. He needed to come home immediately and take care of things.*

*When he arrived at his father's house, sudden sadness and regret filled his heart. He began to search through his father's important papers and saw the small gift-wrapped Bible, just as he had left it years ago. With tears, he opened the Bible and began to turn through the pages. His father had carefully underlined a verse, Matthew 7:11:*
*'And if you, being evil, know how to give good gifts to your children, how much more shall your heavenly Father who is in heaven give to those who ask Him.'*
*As he read those words, a car key dropped from the back of the Bible. It had a tag with the dealer's name on it, the same dealer who had the sports car he desired. On the tag was the date of the graduation and the words PAID IN FULL.*

The thing is, if we're not reaching out into all God has for us, we're selling ourselves short. It is all sitting there waiting for us. We are heirs of the Father, co-heirs with Jesus Christ. That means we inherit our Father's kingdom along with Jesus Christ. It's all ours, not just for when we get to heaven, but NOW, HERE on earth as well. We're rich! We have inherited all of heaven and all of its privileges, freedoms and glorious riches in Christ!

Doesn't that make you excited? All the Father has is ours! But do we live like that, or do we live a life of poverty, spiritually and emotionally? We may know it's ours, but have we actually reached out and received it for ourselves personally?

I know, because I was like that. I was sitting on a goldmine in Christ, and I didn't even know it. My heart is to see you not only come into a place of wholeness but to reach out for all your fullest potential in God. I didn't know my true inheritance in Christ. No one had ever told me. The church I had grown up in never taught me, and I had never searched the scriptures for myself.

God says, *"My people are destroyed through lack of knowledge..." (Hosea 4:6 KJV)*:

- Like Mephibosheth, I was living in rejection, fear, poverty and shame, afraid to come and receive what was rightfully already gifted to me.
- Like the friends of Benny Hinn's great grandparents, sitting on a goldmine, an oil well, and not knowing it.
- Like one of Michelangelo's sculptures, only partially formed, the real me was still locked up in there.
- Like those tractor ruts, in a damaging groove of habits and lifestyle that I needed to get out of.

Please don't be the one who holds back on receiving the indescribable free gift of all Jesus has done for you and walking into the fullness of freedom that is yours. Go and fight for and possess your rightful inheritance! It's all yours! Because of His unconditional love, there is no need to fear or hold back, but bounce up and bounce into all He has to pour into your lap.

Faith is a fight! God had given the Israelites the land, but they still needed to go in and drive out the enemies. Like it or not, we are in the fight of our lives. However, most of us do not even realize that we are in a war, and consequently are not fighting very hard. Some are not resisting at all, believing that everything that comes along is God's will. Faith is not a passive thing. We must rise up and fight for the abundant life God has already given us. I want to implore you with everything within me to RISE UP AND FIGHT!

Our fight is mostly in the spirit and is fought with weapons found in the Word of God. The Bible tells us that the weapons of our warfare are mighty to the pulling down of strongholds. We are told not to tolerate the devil's work in our lives. We are also told not to tolerate doubt, unbelief, and fear. Rather, we are to rise up in faith and kick him out of our lives, and "possess the land" that God has given us. We can do this because we can do all things through Christ who strengthens us.

God has given us great and precious promises, but we must do our part to rise up in the authority of these great promises and "drive out" the enemy by faith. We must develop a hatred for the devil trying to take away the blessings that belong to us. We must rise up with a warrior spirit, born out of the Holy Spirit of God and say, "No, devil, you are not doing this to me. You are not taking this away from me." We need to step outside of our feelings and take an aggressive step of faith in order to destroy the devil's strongholds in our lives.

CONFESSION: I refuse the spirit of self-pity and passivity. I choose to rise up in faith and throw the devil and all of his strongholds out of my life. I will not tolerate his work of doubt and unbelief in my life. I will not tolerate fear. I will seek God's word and God's face, and I will walk in faith. This is my choice, and by the power of the Holy Spirit, I will live in power and victory! I determine to go in and take back what the devil has stolen from me and possess all my rightful inheritance in Jesus Christ!

# KEY 7
## "KNOWING WHO YOU ARE IN GOD"

THE KEY TO a healthy self-image or self-worth is knowing who we are in God. Not relying on what others think or say about us, but knowing what God thinks and says about us. That's all that counts really, isn't it? And the funny thing is, when you feel good about yourself, others do too. Your attitude about yourself either generates friends or turns them away. When you feel good about yourself, the world's your oyster, you feel great, you can do anything! But when you feel bad about yourself, you lash out at others and make mountains out of molehills, all because you don't feel good about yourself. Sound familiar?

Many of us have found our identity in our upbringing, in our work, in our relationships, in our success or lack of it, in our failures, weaknesses, fears and disappointments, in the words that have been spoken over us by the devil, other people and ourselves. There are a host of things that we think make up the total of who we are. Most of them are a false identity and are like shifting sand, unreliable to the point where we can lose our identity and find ourselves in a place of not knowing who we are.

If you identify with this, I encourage you to download the free printable, "Who I am in Christ" from my website or email me for the link. Look up the Scriptures and meditate on them, study them, get to know them well, so that you are absolutely certain how God sees you and who you are in Him. This is imperative.

If you have yet to take the first step of inviting Jesus into your life and accepting Him as your Lord and Saviour, I have included a Prayer of Commitment below. It would give me no greater pleasure than to hear that you have received Christ through reading this book. I would love it if you would email me and let me know.

**Prayer of Salvation**
**DEAR JESUS, I am a sinner and need your forgiveness. I believe You died in my place and rose from the grave to make me new and to prepare me to live in your presence forever. Jesus, please come into my life, take control of my life, forgive my sins and save me. I place my trust in You alone for my salvation, and I accept your free gift of eternal life. AMEN**

# KEY 8
## "FIND YOUR SECURITY IN GOD ALONE"

To LIVE FULLY for God, we must seek to please Him and know our security only in Him. I call it, "living for an audience of One" - living with the awareness of His Presence and His eyes on you. You are secure in His love for you and can do everything for HIS eyes. You'll never be able to please people all the time. I spent my life trying to please people until I discovered this truth:

You can please some of the people some of the time
You can please all of the people some of the time
You can please some of the people all of the time
But you can NEVER please ALL of the people ALL of the time

You will actually wear yourself out trying to please people. When your security is in God alone, however, you need not fear what others think, and it makes no difference whether you succeed or fail. God still loves you completely; therefore, you are also free to take risks in God!

You don't have to prove yourself to God. You are incredibly special to Him. He knows all the things you've been through, and He cares. Live with the awareness that He sees everything, and your quietness and confidence are in Him (Isaiah 30:15). Who you really are (your character) is who you are when no one is looking.

Live your life giving Him the highest honour, developing incredible gratitude and a healthy fear of God, not getting familiar because the things of God are sacred. Hold them in highest honour. This will keep you walking lightly before Him - practising His Presence – which to me is the ultimate secret.

Know Him. What is He like? What is His nature? Finding personal security and worth in God alone is the only thing that can truly free a person to be who they were meant to be.

> *"You made all the delicate inner parts of my body and knit them together in my mother's womb. Thank you for making me so wonderfully complex! It is amazing to think about. Your workmanship is marvellous - and how well I know it. You were there while I was being formed in utter seclusion! You saw me before I was born and scheduled each day of my life before I began to breathe. Every day was recorded in your Book! How precious it is, Lord, to realize that you are thinking about me constantly! I can't even count how many times a day your thoughts turn towards me. And when I wake in the morning, you are still thinking of me!" (Psalm 139:13-18)*

Since the Father, Jesus, and the Holy Spirit are totally perfect in their natures and have no dark side to their personalities, then they, and only they, are the Ones who are capable of giving you a perfect, pure, and unconditional love that no one else can give you in this life. This is why the Bible tells us that we will find a peace that will pass all human understanding once we have accepted Jesus as our personal Lord and Savior and have become truly born again. That peace we will find is the result of finding the one true Person who can fill the empty void within us - and that one Person is God Almighty Himself. (There is a prayer you can pray to accept Jesus as your personal Lord and Saviour under "Knowing Who You Are in God".)

There are two critical keys, the two most important things in life that will be our sure foundation in finding our security. They are **'Knowing God'** and **'Knowing Who You Are in Him'**. The growing realisation of who God is and who you are in God is truly liberating in every area of your life. I have found throughout the years, time and time again through the crucible of trials when things are extra tough or uncertain, the people or things I thought were dependable turned out not to be. There's been painful betrayal, my heart has been broken, or the rug has been pulled out from under my feet. But these are the two CERTAIN things that you can hold onto and are your sure foundation. They will hold you steady in the face of all hell breaking loose around you and are so critically important. Knowing God...and being sure of your identity in Him.

The names of God in the Word tell us a lot of what He is like, his nature. This is so crucial for you to find your security in Him. To really know His nature, not just what you have heard or think you know. To know without a doubt who He is. (You can download a free printable from my website on "Knowing God" or I will gladly send it if you email me..) Study the Word for yourself, look up the scriptures, and it will change your life. You will find yourself feeling so much more secure, and your prayer life will change. The amazing thing is when you know how much you are loved, and when you know God's nature and heart toward you, you can entrust yourself so much more to His protection and care, therefore relieving your fear and stress.

That must be why the Bible teaches that *"those who KNOW their God will be strong and do exploits." (Daniel 11:32).* We are made to know God – to know ABOUT Him and to know Him PERSONALLY, as a Father, as a Friend, and as our Creator and Sustainer. When we don't know God, we don't really know anything. Our lives are as incomplete without Him as a sky without a sun.

*"My soul finds rest in God alone." (Psalm 62:1)*

When our souls find rest in Him ALONE, the most important thing in life is not ...

- what we do,
- where we go,
- who we're with,
- how high we rise,
- how long we live, or
- how influential we become.

The most important thing in life is HIM. When we don't trust God, it's a sign we don't truly know Him.

Our default tendency is to trust in ourselves and lean on our own understanding. But when we encounter a problem that's bigger than our ability to handle – that's when we learn our own resources are inadequate and that we can't truly rely on Jesus until we stop trying to rely only on ourselves. Nothing compares with getting to know the God who knows us and finding our security (present and eternal) in Him alone.

Be more God-conscious, and you'll be less self-conscious!

# KEY 9
## "CANCEL THE PITY PARTIES"

YOU KNOW THE ones - where you invite Me, Myself and I over and you get down and negative and depressing together. "Woe is me! The world sucks! Everything sucks!"

It hit me between the eyeballs one day when I learnt that self-pity is a sin. I was shocked! I had been giving myself permission to sin in this way. Once I had that knowledge, I had to repent and ask for forgiveness.

Don't allow yourself to wallow in self-pity. If you're prone to getting depressed, don't allow yourself to get into self-pity because it's always a downward spiral. It drains your body physically, which makes you more depressed and drained, which makes you more depressed; it's a vicious circle. I had to stop focusing on self and instead set my mind on Jesus. I set myself lists of things to do so that I had no time to think about myself.

One of the things that happens when you are in a depressed place is you get very locked in. I often had to shake my head and literally make my eyes focus on something external. It was like shaking myself out of myself. We get too locked into me, me, me. How about helping others in need? For example, we only need to visit a hospital ward for an afternoon and to soon realize our problems are small.

Forgetting about feelings and just throwing yourself into a goal can help to take our eyes off ourselves. You can make lists of things to do and cross them off when you've done them. Starting to get things back in order and staying organized is a mood lifter because when things at home begin to fall down, these are prime conditions for depression and are also signs of depression.

I MADE myself get up and start crossing those things off my list. It gave me another focus. It got me out of myself and "the doing" of those things also gave me a great sense of achievement and further motivation. If you're that sort of person, always have another goal on up ahead, so you can throw yourself into that when this one's finished.

When we lived in Whakatane, on the way to Ohope, we passed a road to the dump. We would often go there if we had loads of garden waste and other rubbish to take there. It was a smelly place at the end of a dead-end road, and you could get your car bogged in the mud there easily. That is what it is like when you turn down the road of discouragement and self-pity. We learned to just not turn down the Discouragement Road, because it was like the road to the dump. There was nothing nice down there, just rubbish, and you could easily get bogged. It is hard to get out of. So, just stay on the main road, don't even turn into Discouragement Road because there is nothing nice to see down there.

I love Joyce Meyer's teaching on "A Wandering Mind" from her book, "The Battlefield of the Mind." I like to explain it like this: when you find your mind wandering down the wrong tracks (as it regularly does), you just need to whistle it back, like you're whistling a wandering dog. Tell it to "heel", "Get in behind." Don't let it wander off into all the wrong places. Don't allow yourself to get bogged in a victim mentality.

# KEY 10
## "DADDY'S GIRL"

Every little girl looks for validation, admiration and love from her father. She looks to him for her self-worth and to tell her she is beautiful. That is the way God has made her. When she hasn't received that as a little girl, she is left abandoned, like an orphan.

Being abandoned, violated or abused by a father causes a little girl (and boys too) to have trouble with their view of God as Father. I hadn't realized that my longing for validation from him was keeping me stuck.

I remember it dawning on me, one day when I was crying out to God for an answer to a particular prayer, that because my own father had stood aside and not stepped in to help me or stand up for me, I had a similar subconscious view of my Heavenly Father. Perhaps He was standing off, holding out on me and not going to step in to help me? Perhaps He might not be there for me when I really needed Him? Maybe I wasn't valuable enough for Him, or maybe He got some strange satisfaction out of seeing me suffer? Maybe He wasn't reliable or trustworthy?

I didn't believe it in my mind because the Word of God told me differently, but somewhere deep in my psyche, it was there. The issue was how I related to God the Father. Was He really going to protect me? Could I really trust Him completely? Did He really want to give me good things and spoil me as His daughter?

I had no trouble believing my Creator All-Powerful God or my loving self-sacrificing Saviour Jesus or my Personal Helper and Counsellor Holy Spirit. It was the Father concept of God that maybe had been tainted and needed a little work. My "little girl heart," deep inside, wanted to believe the truth desperately (and I'm sure she did) but was being held back to draw closer to her Heavenly Father by the way she had been treated by her own earthly father.

We had been singing a beautiful song at church called "He's a Good, Good Father," by Chris Tomlin. One day, while that song was playing in my worship time at home, I began declaring in the Spirit all the things that the best father would be like, and thanking God that this was who He is, what He is like and more. At the same time, I started declaring all the things that He was not like. This went on for some time, and it was like He and I together were caught up in the Spirit. Out of the depths of my being came the cry of my heart that released all that betrayal and disappointment from my earthly father and received the pure, untainted, sanctified, unconditional, holy love from my Heavenly Father, who is fiercely jealous over me and loves me with an everlasting fiery passion. Tears ran freely; tears of release, tears of healing and tears of joy. I know the Holy Spirit did a great healing work that day, so powerful that it makes me cry when I think about it even now. He truly is the good good Father! And I am free to be My Father's daughter - I have to say, I'm a real Daddy's girl!

I would encourage you as the Holy Spirit leads, to take some time to connect with your Heavenly Father in a similar way. It is so powerful! So many times, we can do, see, achieve and become, yet none of it will ever come close to being loved by the One who is Perfect Holy Love. Love is more powerful than we think! It can change who we are. I no longer need to love by keeping an empty set of rules. I don't have to perform for Him or keep Him happy. Perfect Love changes your heart!

# KEY 11
## "HE LOVES ME; HE LOVES ME NOT"

DID YOU EVER play, "He loves me, He loves me not" with daisy petals as a child or teenager? As you worked your way around the flower, picking off each petal and letting it fall to the ground, supposedly whichever was the last phrase on the last petal told you if that boy you liked, loved you back.

We often find ourselves picking through the circumstances and things that happen in our lives, like little children plucking daisy petals, attempting to figure out whether or not God loves us. When everything is going well, you feel loved. When hard things come your way, you begin to wonder if maybe He doesn't love you as much as He loves others or has stopped loving you. This can be especially so when you have grown up with a parent or controlling figure who withholds love unless you measure up to their expectations. When you feel like you're doing well and measuring up, you feel loved. But when you fail or get it wrong, or know you're not making it, you wonder again if you are even loveable. If you, like me, have found yourself least certain of His love in those critical moments when you need Him most, there is hope for you.

**Where?** At the one event in human history that forever secured your place in the Father's heart – the cross, where Jesus allowed sin and shame to be consumed in His own body so that you could freely embrace a relationship with His Father. If that is not true love, then what is? Jesus died for YOU! The Father loved you so much, He was willing to pay the highest price that could ever be paid - His only Son, His absolute best and perfect sacrifice. And at the cross, you will discover that what God always wanted was not the fearful subservience of slaves or the exemplary performance of puppets, but the loving affection of, and fellowship with, sons and daughters.

In Him, you will find…

- A Father who loves you more than anyone on this planet ever has or ever will;
- A growing confidence in His affection for you through whatever circumstances you face;
- A vibrant relationship with Him that will free you from the torment of shame and rejection, while it transforms you to live as His child in the earth.

His love is:

- unconditional,
- unmerited,
- undeserved,
- unlimited (measureless).

That's the best part - all we have to do is receive it. It is freely given and freely received.

Learning to receive His love and trust Him fully is not something any of us can resolve in an instant; it's something we'll grow to discover for the whole of our lives as we get to know His nature and who we are in Him. God knows how difficult it is for us to accept His love, and He teaches us with more patience than we've ever known. Through every circumstance and in the most surprising ways, He makes His love known to us in ways we can understand.

It's time to toss your daisies aside and discover that it is not the fear of losing God's love that will keep us on His path, but THE SIMPLE JOY OF LIVING IN IT EVERY DAY.

*"How great is the love the Father has lavished on us,*
*that we should be called children of God! And that is what we are!*
*(1 John 3:1)*

# KEY 12
## "LOVE BEING YOU"

ALL OF US would find it far easier to write a list of ten negative things about ourselves than positive ones. We could do that speedily, no problem at all, especially all our physical faults. But when people are asked to write ten positive things about themselves, they immediately struggle.

I hated myself so much as a child and then even more in my twenties, as I struggled to find myself after all that had happened. Most of us have a negative self-image due to the fall, until we come to know Jesus Christ, but some of us have a particularly low image, or even self-loathing or self-hatred, due to various environments, people, experiences or adverse things that have happened to us.

Accepting yourself and loving who you are automatically changes what you attract, tolerate, and allow into your life. I have noticed that as little children who are brought up in a positive home environment with a healthy view of themselves go off to school, it doesn't take them long to start to realize that maybe not everyone is going to like them, and they start to become more self-conscious. It is amazing how fast that happens, to varying degrees of course. The world is very good at knocking us down to size, so for those who haven't had a positive upbringing and are perhaps experiencing ongoing bullying or abuse at home, any adverse treatment they receive out in the world is just piling damage upon damage.

We also have different personality types, and some of us are more sensitive personality types than others. Learning about the different personality types can be hugely releasing for people, as they all of a sudden realize why they are like they are. I encourage you to learn more about personality types as it can help you not only understand yourself but value your strengths.

During my journey, I became more aware of the fact that I hated myself. For as long as I could remember, I had. Here I was, heading for 30 years of age, and I hated myself. In the years I was in the workforce and met and married my husband, I gained some self-worth, but still, if you asked me, I would say I didn't like myself. When depression, shame and the sense of being a failure came to the surface, it just made me hate myself even more.

I remember the day on my journey out of depression when I finally plucked up the courage to do as a book had suggested and tell myself that I loved myself. "I love me" – it was such a hard thing to say. I remember it vividly to this day. It really stuck in my throat. I kept persevering, and gradually I could start to say it a bit louder and more confidently, and even look in the mirror and say it.

I had to learn that God doesn't make junk! God must have known what He was doing when He made me. He made me one-of-a-kind, uniquely me. And He liked the "me" He made. Who was I to criticise His workmanship? By criticising myself and putting myself down, I was in effect, criticising His handiwork and His choices! It was He who carefully and precisely crafted me and knitted me together in seclusion, adding all my different personality traits, my looks, my fair skin, my likes, dislikes and preferences. I needed to start liking the "me" He had made, and to stop wishing or hoping I could be someone else.

Not only did I need to start liking myself, but I also needed to start enjoying and celebrating who He had made me and **being the best ME I could be** with what He had given me. To be able to laugh at myself and my funny little ways, instead of trying to be perfect, was a huge breakthrough. This took some time, but finally I began to feel comfortable in my own skin, realizing I belonged to Him all along and I was His choice to make this way (freckles, fair Irish skin and all).

This revelation gave me great value and dignity. I am made in the very image of my Creator God. Wow! He has placed parts of Himself in me and breathed into me His very breath of life. And if that is not enough, He has chosen me, redeemed me, restored me, made me a whole new creation, come to dwell in me, and placed His Holy Spirit, His very glory in me.

Jesus had this remarkable perception when he offered the commandment to "love others as we love ourselves." If we can't love ourselves, how on earth are we going to truly be able to love other people? People who don't like themselves, or don't feel good about themselves tend to be very down on and critical of others. That appears to be a subconscious way of trying to boost themselves. We have always noticed with our girls growing up that whenever they weren't feeling very good about themselves, they would start playing up or picking at their siblings. That usually triggered us having some one-on-one time with them privately (away from the others) to see what was triggering this and what was really going on in their life.

Dr Robert Schuller teaches (in his book, *"Self Love")*: "Every negative thinker I have ever met distrusts himself, belittles himself, and downgrades himself." This lack of self-worth lies at the root of almost every one of our personal problems. I remember producing an assignment on this at Bible College, and it became one of my keen interests when I realized it was at the root of all our social ills. Because of that, it is also something I have worked on tirelessly with my own girls and been at the base of all our ministry over the years. Dr Schuller goes on to say:

> *"When you challenge an impossibility thinker to become a possibility thinker, and they answer somewhat predictably, "It's not worth the effort" - what they are really meaning is "I'm not worth it." What you need to do is go to work on building up in their mind a picture of their enormous worth as a person. Then, little by little, when they begin to stop hating themselves and start liking themselves, they come alive. They become a possibility thinker." (Dr Robert Schuller)*

No matter what has happened in your life, you are NOT "a *complete* failure, a *hopeless* sinner, a *total* washout". That exaggerated, distorted, destructive lie has been repeated thousands of times. In every instance, you will be able to point out worthwhile qualities in the person who was condemning themselves unfairly, unreasonably, and unlovingly.

It's up to you to give your self-respect a boost! Other people will not respect you if you don't respect yourself. If you run yourself down, you'll soon have those who would boost you believing you are right, and they are wrong. You need to learn how to become your own best friend. **To love yourself is to be truly Christian!**

It IS a sin not to love what God loves! The Bible teaches that God loves every person. No person will love God so long as he fails to love himself.

Self-love is the ultimate hunger or will of humans - that's what we really want more than anything else in the world - the awareness that we are worthy. It is the deepest of all the currents which drive us onward, forward and upward. All other drives - pleasure, power, love, meaning, creativity - are symptoms, expressions or attempts to fulfil that primal need for personal dignity.

As infants, we learn that we love and are usually loved in return, which leaves us with a wonderful feeling of wellbeing. We fail to perceive that this sense of wellbeing is really an experience of self-love, so we go through life driven by the compulsion to love - unaware that what we really seek is not love as an end in itself, but as food to nourish our self-love. Again, we discover, early in life, that a wonderful feeling of wellbeing sweeps over us when we love other people. We fail to analyse our feelings precisely enough if we stop short of labelling that sense of wellbeing what it really is - self-love.

So, the will to love and to be loved is a compulsion either to share our strong self-love or to support our own shaky self-love.

You are on the road to emotional, mental and spiritual health when you discover that what you really want more than anything else in life is neither survival pleasure, power, love, or meaning. **What you really want is to be able to know and appreciate yourself!**

Victor Frankl was asked: "If it is true that all living organisms have evolved from a slimy amoeba in a swampy pool, and if the human being is the highest form of this purely natural evolution, can you tell me how the human being ever evolved into a creature that demands dignity? Why, of all organisms, does the human being have this craving for dignity, self-respect and self-love?"

"The answer to that question," he replied, "is one I really don't know." Psychologists and psychiatrists and scientists alike don't want to admit it, but the truth is that we are this way because we are the reflections of God, just as surely as the moon is the reflection of the sun.

The Psalmist had the answer when he wrote, *"Man was made in the image of God, just a little lower than the angels." (Psalm 8:5; Genesis 1:27; Genesis 5:1).* According to the Bible, the first human being was created in the image of God - with the urge to be creative, a desire to act gloriously, and a compulsion to live life on a grand scale. So, God placed man in charge of God's ordered creation, to rule, exercise dominion and be the great decision-making creatures. Man was a supreme display of dignity incarnate! He was the star of God's creation!

This urge for greatness, the compulsion to create, the passion for excellence, the desire for recognition, the discontent with imperfection, the demand for personal freedom, the need to give and receive love, even the desire to rule and dominate - all originate with our ancestral divine heritage when God made man to be great, glorious and perfectly awesome!

When a man senses that he is near greatness, at the beginning of something big, at the edge of glory, at the brink of success, on the stairway to stardom, his heart beats fast and his blood stirs, his pulse pounds with happy anticipation! For he was born for greatness! We sense that we were born for something bigger and better than we know today. We keep moving restlessly onward and upward, seeking a dignity we instinctively know is our heritage.

**You have no idea what a tremendous person you can be if you will only believe in yourself! A deep sense of self-worth gives rise to self-confidence. This, in turn, produces the drive that leads a person to success. After all, what is self-confidence but the belief in one's ability to succeed over difficulties? Self-love produces a power that shrivels mountains into molehills.**

# KEY 13
## "WORD BEFORE WORLD"

MAKE THIS YOUR resolve - to put the "Word Before the World". We can have an unhealthy pattern of waking up and scrolling our phones in the first moments of the day. We can excuse this scroll as time to help our body wake up, but the Lord knows that at the bottom of our scrolling is a heart of laziness and a lack of discipline.

Elisabeth Elliot says: "**Discipline is the wholehearted yes to the call of God.** When I know myself called, summoned, addressed, taken possession of, known, acted upon, I have heard the Master. I put myself gladly, fully, and forever at His disposal, and to whatever He says, my answer is Yes."

The first moments of our day shape the rest of it, and yet too often we allow the things of this world to become more alluring and exciting than the Word of God. Decide, by the grace of God, to put the Word back in its proper, first place.

Be aware that the morning, when you first awaken, can be the most difficult time to set your mind right – the battle for your mind has already started. When you wake up, say out loud a scripture that encourages you. Learn to start your day right and **SET YOUR MIND.** A favorite Scripture for me in the morning is: *This is the day the Lord has made, I will rejoice and be glad in it.* (Psalm 118:24) Another great one is this: *Be diligent in setting your mind daily on things above that are eternal, not the things of this world that are temporary. (Colossians 3:12)*

You need the Word of God first thing... before everything else starts taking precedence in your mind. I used to have a personal motto which said, "No Word, No Breakfast." In other words, if I hadn't been in the Word, I would forfeit my breakfast time to get into the Word instead. Nowadays, you could make it "No Word, No Phone". We say we have no time, yet we find time to spend endlessly scrolling our phones, and before we know it, half an hour, an hour, even two hours have gone by, invested in something which is here today, forgotten tomorrow.

*"Man does not live by bread alone,*
*but by every Word that proceeds from the mouth of God."*
*(Matt 4:4)*

*"I have treasured the words of his mouth more than my daily food."*
*(Job 23:12)*

With the increase of technological advancement in our society has come a host of other distractions and addictions. We live in a day and age where our screens have become more important than our God. Rewiring our fingers and brains to go to Jesus before the world will not only change our days, it will revolutionise our lives because the Bible is the living, breathing, always active words of God! It is written for our instruction and encouragement. It gives us life, comfort, direction and everything that we need for each day.

Why would we give our hearts to the things of this world that dishearten, discourage and distract, when we have the actual words of God that are unchanging and never fail, ready to be digested by our hearts and minds? Everything of this world is temporary, whereas the Word of God will last forever! Everything of this world is like sinking sand and can't be relied upon, whereas the Word of God is our sure foundation. It grounds us. Everything of this world is feeding us a mixture of lies and truth that we constantly have to filter, whereas the Word of God is pure unadulterated truth – we can get into it and just devour it all with no filter. Everything in this world is spinning our minds all over the place, whereas the Word of God brings peace and stability, security, reliability, certainty, hope and calm.

The Word of God is the center of gravity around which our world orbits. Without it, first thing in the day, our world is spinning every which way but loose.

Once we taste of the goodness of Jesus Christ, the Living Word Himself, the rest of the world will lose its flavour. Pick up your fork and taste Jesus. Dig into the Word of God to know just how good it tastes.

There is no end of helpful apps with Bible reading plans or devotionals for each day. But again, if you are addicted and distracted by your phone, you may do better with a printed book format. Get yourself one from your local Christian bookstore or online. What matters is that you diligently seek God through His Word, not how much you ingest each day. Quality trumps quantity! (If you need help in choosing a good one, feel free to email me for a list of suggestions.)

Putting the "**Word Before the World**" in your life will redefine your attitudes and perspectives in life, and it will prepare you with the ammunition you need to fight the fight of faith. **Knowing Jesus is more important than knowing what's happened overnight on Instagram or Facebook.**

Consider waking up to an alarm clock rather than your phone, to remove the temptation of checking your email, reading the news, responding to texts, or scrolling social media first thing. No matter what your mornings look like, choose at least one verse to meditate on first thing. If you can get up and have your time with Jesus in those first moments, praise the Lord! Guard those moments and make them a priority!

I know there are many of you for whom having a quiet time first thing is truly not possible, but you can still make it a priority to set your mind on Jesus in those first moments. If you can't have your full quiet time, I guarantee you have just a few minutes in which you could read a Psalm or meditate on one verse. Maybe choose a verse to memorise each month, and that's the verse you meditate on as you cook breakfast, go for a run or walk, or take a shower. You could even print off certain scriptures, laminate them and place them around the area where you shower or put on your makeup. Use that time to think about scripture and hide it in your heart. You could even use a dry erase marker to write scriptures on your mirror. Think outside the box! I used to plaster them everywhere - they were my absolute lifeline!

*"Listen carefully to my words.*
*Do not let them out of your sight, keep them within your heart."*
*(Proverbs 4:20-21)*

*"Now set your mind and heart to seek, inquire of and require as your vital necessity the Lord your God."*
*(1 Chronicles 22:19 AMP)*

Even with four young children (including a breastfed baby), this was SO IMPORTANT to me – I could not survive without the Word in my life. I hung onto it for dear life. It is living and active and continued to work in my life throughout my day. That meant setting myself a schedule where I would get up in the morning half an hour before they were all awake (my husband was usually still out milking the cows) and grab my Bible and my journal. That generally gave me uninterrupted time, which was "my time" before the rush of the day came crashing in on me. Often, I felt so tired and I could hardly pull myself out of bed, but I knew that if I didn't do it then, I would miss my opportunity and I would be on the back foot all day. I literally had to do it, as my vital necessity. "Where there is a will, there is a way." Put your feet over the side of the bed, and the rest of your body will follow.

Evaluate your schedule and your heart motives. Quit the excuses. We've got to teach our hearts and minds and souls that Jesus is more important than social media, than the world. We can't live without Him, but we can certainly live without Facebook or Instagram or the news.

He is where your answer lies. Get into the Word of God as if your life depended on it - because it actually does! Choose the better portion, which will last forever. That time in the Word of God and in

His presence is where you will find your courage to go into your day rising up to be all you can be in God.

"Courage is fear that has said its prayers."

# KEY 14
## "EXERCISE AND HEALTH ARE KEY"

Stress produces a lot of adrenalin and cortisol in our system. Adrenalin is released in our body, getting it ready for a "fight" or "flight" response. In brief, it's a survival mechanism, enabling us to react quickly to life-threatening situations. A stressful situation can trigger a cascade of stress hormones that produce physiological changes. It can make the heart pound and breathing quicken; muscles tense and beads of sweat appear. One wrong thought can send us into stress mode, and unfortunately, the body can also overreact to stressors that are not life-threatening, such as traffic jams, work pressure and family difficulties. The more stressed we get; the more is released. Long-term stress takes a huge toll on the body. We are not made to live at high stress all the time, with high levels of stress hormones in our system. We need to interrupt short-term stress with times of rest and equilibrium.

If the adrenalin is not used up by working it off, it becomes like a poisonous toxin in our system, which makes us sluggish and depressed. Some experts say it is like rust; it corrodes or rusts out our system. You're high one day and low the next. So, the more we're under stress, the more we need to exercise to work it out of our system.

Exercise is vital as it not only releases these stress hormones out of our system, it also has the bonus of releasing endorphins (the "feel good" chemicals), which trigger a positive feeling in your body, like that of morphine. I started getting outside and having a good old jump on the kid's trampoline. It was fun, as well as exhilarating and a good workout. I didn't feel like it, especially at first, but I made myself do it, again by faith. Being outside with the vast wide expanse of the sky above, or the vast expanse of the sea and waves gets you out of that small, locked-in feeling. Don't stay inside with the blinds pulled but get out from under those ceilings above your head.

## Stop the Sugar Binges

I know all about the low blood sugar, triggered by the carbohydrate and sugar binges, that comes from eating for comfort. Once you start, you can't stop. They're the worst. You go way up, then crash way down.

A quote from J.J. Virgin might be worth considering: "A classic sign of a food intolerance is craving the very food that is hurting you." We tend to binge food that is doping our systems. Healthy fats and proteins can curb your appetite and make sweets far less tempting. There is much written on healthy eating today, and there are plenty of resources available, so that is all I will say on the matter here.

Most people by now know the benefits of drinking plenty of water rather than sugary drinks or alcohol. Think of your body like a high-performance engine that needs the best fuel put into it to make it perform at its best.

## Get a Health Check

I understand that something as simple as a thyroid imbalance can cause low mood or depression. Also, a Vitamin D deficiency can play a part through lack of sunlight. You can ask your doctor for a simple test to check all is well there. You could also ask a natural health professional for advice on vitamin or mineral deficiencies.

Discovering a Vitamin B deficiency was a huge key for me, and nowadays it is interesting to note that more health experts are starting to discover magnesium deficiency also can trigger or be a cause of depression, fatigue and anxiety disorders. Many are finding great success in treating depression and anxiety disorders with Vitamin B6 plus magnesium.

There is no harm in checking these things out, if you haven't already, then at least you have ruled out any physical cause. I would recommend taking a Vitamin B complex and magnesium anyway, to boost your brain health and nervous system while you fight your way back to recovery. Again, there are plenty of resources available for you to do your own research but don't become a hypochondriac like I did. Have your checks or tests to rule out anything physical, but then get on and deal with the spiritual keys and thought processes that will catapult you back to good health. As I have said elsewhere, if you give your body the right environment, it is amazing at healing itself.

# 🔍 KEY 15
## "A PROSPEROUS SOUL"

SOME OF US are very good at looking after everyone else, but not so good at taking care of ourselves. This is especially true of those with a self-sacrificing nature.

We need to learn not only to replenish our **Physical Tank** (with food, sleep, exercise, water, fresh air), and our **Spiritual Tank** (with the Bible, prayer, church, etc), but, and this is an area most people neglect, we need to look after our **Emotional Tank** (our soul).

We are tri-partite beings made up of body, soul and spirit. When one of the three areas is not doing well, it is not in unity with the rest of us, creating a war or stress or disease in our whole wellbeing.

What are the things that replenish your emotional tank? What things are therapeutic for you? For some, it is a long luxurious bubble bath with a good book or a long walk on the beach. For others, it is gardening or going for a run (that sounds like work to me). For others, it is hanging out with their favourite people at a café, shopping or watching a good movie. Whatever it is for you, make sure you schedule time to replenish your soul and refill your emotional tank. Just as you wouldn't let the battery run right down on your phone without recharging it, don't let this happen to you either. Self-care is a priority, not a luxury.

I used to go hard at things and then crash in a big heap because I forgot to look after myself in the process. Learn to pace yourself, especially in the busy times. Make sure you add margin to your schedule, so you have time to replenish your emotional tank. These margins should be added as "part of" your work, not as an addition or only when you have time for them - "If you fail to plan, you plan to fail."

Practising self-care is about fighting your way back to a prosperous soul, no matter what you go through. Process things as you go, in prayer, with your Counsellor, the Holy Spirit. Some of us are real "stuffers" - we just keep stuffing stuff down on the inside and not taking time to process it as we go. Keep short accounts (like the dirt on your floor, it doesn't do any good to keep sweeping it under the mat, or you will end up with a big pile to deal with). Keep your soul free from carrying heavy weights or excess baggage (like irritations, disappointments or conflicts with people) because those are a huge drain emotionally. Keeping your soul prospering is paramount.

This was a key for us raising four children while in ministry. Pastors and leaders' kids (in fact, all kids) can experience all kinds of disappointments when working with people. People get into conflicts, take offense, have disagreements, lash out against leaders, leave churches, spread rumours and lies, and a whole host of other things. It happens in business, it happens in politics, it happens no matter what group you are a part of, and it also, sadly, happens in the church. Many children will become disillusioned and leave church if we don't help them process things along the way. If they keep stuffing things, they will end up with their soul not prospering, which will eventually affect their spiritual life and everything else. It is absolutely key to help them keep their soul free and prospering.

A prosperous soul produces life and prosperity around you; whereas a defeated soul produces death and defeat around you. Your life reproduces on the outside what it is on the inside. People say you have to be real (as if real is pouring out the negative). A prosperous soul IS real, pouring from the inside of you! When your soul is prospering, all is right with the world (even amongst the challenges).

Keeping your soul prospering is about managing yourself well - your marriage and family health, your financial health, and your emotional health. When those aren't managed well, they are a huge draw off on your emotional tank.

For me, the bottom line is whether my relationship with God is flourishing. Is my marriage flourishing? Are my family relationships flourishing? There will be times when it appears the bottom has dropped out in your life. At the end of the day, you can sustain everything else if those things are intact – you mustn't lose sight of them.

Closely related to a prosperous soul is disappointing the devil by bouncing back, no matter what gets thrown at you. Being rooted and grounded in the right things (the things you are learning here) so you're not easily offended, and not dwelling on failures and setbacks. You get knocked down, but you get back up again. You're determined to bounce back, pull yourself up by the bootstraps and keep on going. You know where your confidence and security are, and you can, like David, encourage yourself in the Lord even when there are no other encouragers around you - *"Then after the battle you will still be standing firm." (Ephesians 6:13)*

Don't beat yourself up if you have some down days. Just get back up, dust yourself off, get your thinking right and keep going. No matter what you go through, fight your way back to that prosperous soul.

*"Beloved, I pray that you may prosper in all things and be in health,*
*just as your soul prospers."*
*(3 John 1:2 KJV)*

You may not have any official letters after your name, but you CAN give yourself permission to put two letters after your name: **B.A. = "Bounceback Ability."**

# KEY 16
## "FUN AND LAUGHTER"

*"A merry heart does good like a medicine,*
*but a broken spirit dries the bones."*
(Prov 17:22)

JUST AS NEGATIVE, self-centred thinking is draining to our body, the Word of God is like healing to the body. Laughter is good!

I once heard the true story of a man with a terminal illness, who shut himself away in a room with funny movies and laughed himself silly. He got better! Our bodies are so fantastically made. Did you know every cell in our body is replaced over a period of seven years? Given the right conditions, our bodies can heal themselves. But the only way we'll have the exact right conditions is as we abide in Christ. A negative attitude is so draining to our physical bodies, which in turn affects our mental health, whereas giving our bodies a positive, uplifting attitude is the perfect environment for health to flourish and heal itself, including any imbalances. There is so much more research being done on this today - these things I had to learn the hard way.

So, get some fun back into your life! Hang out with fun people. Watch funny movies and let the laughter out. Do some fun activities, roll on the ground laughing with your friend, partner or kids. Have some good belly laughs. Find the silly and let that laughter bring health to you - body, soul and spirit. It is so, so good for you! When life feels like it is getting far too serious, it is time to hang out with some people who are fun to be with and just have heaps of laughs. It is a great stress reliever.

# KEY 17
# LEARN BETTER WAYS OF MANAGING STRESS

## Pressure isn't all bad.

Pressure is good in that it brings things to the surface that need to be dealt with. The real you comes out under pressure. But we need to process those things properly and move on, not leave them stuffed down on the inside.

As I got older, all the stuff from my childhood that I had just stuffed down inside started coming up and needed to be dealt with. Over the last 30 years, wherever I have spoken, people understand exactly what I am saying. Apart from those in the younger age brackets, I have been astounded at the number of 40, 50, 60, and even 70-year-olds who ask for prayer, telling me that they have never talked about their past issues with anyone, and never dealt with childhood abuse or major unforgiveness. Many of those have also suffered a number of nervous breakdowns.

If you don't deal with these things, they will start surfacing in your 20's, and if you don't deal with them then, they will try and resurface again in your 30's, or your 40's and so on – especially when you are under pressure. These issues must come up and out and be dealt with once and for all. You cannot just keep the lid on them - just like a pressure cooker, they will blow the valve.

## Stress isn't all bad

No stress at all would be boring. It is part of life. It's learning how to handle the stress that matters. You've probably already learned that there is good stress and bad stress. "Fight or flight" stress that gets you going when you are in danger and need to act, for example, is helpful. Stress that motivates you is good. But none of us is built to live under prolonged stress constantly. Our bodies are made to ebb and flow with the level of stress hormones in our body elevated for when required, but then to ease back to a place of rest in between times. Even high-performance athletes know that they can push their bodies to extreme stress for a period of time, but then they need to ease back to a place of rest. If they don't, their bodies will become worn out or overloaded.

The female system and metabolism are very sensitive to stress. Stress can set off a whole chain-reaction which affects almost every part of our system, causing an imbalance in our hormones, our digestive systems and in so many different areas.

When your body releases stress hormones like adrenaline, it turns on your "monkey mind" (that worrying part of your brain that won't shut up). If you're under a lot of stress, you need to learn how to channel it in the right direction by the way that you think.

## Take the breaks off

When you work - work well! But when you rest - rest well! Let everything regularly come back to a proper equilibrium, to a restful place. God gave us a day of rest in our week, but today, many of us fill that up to the brim with stressful activities and work as well.

One way we can ease stress in our life is to go with the pressure (in our thinking) – to go with the flow. Don't fight it, don't pull against. I call it "**taking your foot off the brakes in your head**." It is like you are driving along at 100 miles per hour, but you've got your foot on the brakes unconsciously in your head. You're pulling against the stress and getting all tense. Do you know what happens when you drive your car like that, with the brakes on? It will burn the brakes out!

Stress is caused by two things pulling in opposite directions. Did you know that's the way to test steel, in a bridge for example, is to put it under great stress? So, don't pull against it – go with it. Let the brakes off. Don't see problems as a negative and start complaining but see problems as a challenge to overcome and to be victorious over. "Great, we've got a problem. Let's you and I work it out together." Ask the creative "how". For every problem, there is a solution. In that way, you can make stress work for you. Don't fight it. When we start pulling back, it creates a real tug-o-war inside and causes your nerves to tense up like a tight rubber band. Let God show you the positive things in each situation.

There was one day where we had a family staying with us. It had been a particularly busy season, and I was looking for a break in the whirlwind. We had an event until late the evening before and a Saturday morning breakfast meeting in the city the next morning. We rushed home in gridlock traffic for a quick bite of lunch with our kids, who had been left with our visitors, got dressed up for a wedding, said our quick goodbyes to them all leaving our guests to pack themselves up and make their own departure, and we raced off on a two-hour trip to Tauranga for our niece's wedding. We would need to travel back late that night for a full day of Sunday services and people ministry the next day! We were travelling along at 100 km per hour (ever feel like life is like that sometimes?) and I felt like the "brakes were on in my head". I could have done without this long trip there and back for a wedding. I was feeling the stress - like two things were pulling in opposite directions, and I was resisting it.

My husband reminded me to see it as an adventure. And as soon as I did that, I released the "brakes in my head" and let go to enjoy the crazy ride. It made all the difference. How do you ride a rollercoaster? Certainly not with your feet on the brakes. You sit back and enjoy the twists and turns and exhilarating crazy ride. And we thoroughly enjoyed our time chatting together along the journey, our time with family and the late trip home again for a big Sunday. The stress and pressure were relieved, all because I made a choice to see it differently and let go.

If your problems start getting too much, that is a sure sign that you need to take some time to recuperate, refresh and recharge. Key signs are that you don't want to answer another email or take another phone call, or you start avoiding people or situations. Take notice of those signs; you won't be able to keep rising to challenges if you are so depleted. It's amazing how everything looks so different after some rest and relaxation (see "Prosperous Soul" and "Relaxation Techniques" for tips on this).

If there is literally no gap for you to take time out, then learn how to do what I call "refuelling mid-flight". Take small moments of five, ten or thirty-minute holidays along the way and maximise them. In other words, add some spice, some fun, some laughter, some little margins into your schedule, which will help relieve the pressure and help you enjoy the journey more.

"Remember that stress doesn't come from what's going on in your life.
It comes from your thoughts about what's going on in your life."
(Andrew J Bernstein)

## Lean into the Holy Spirit

Another key which I find extremely helpful is "leaning into the Holy Spirit". When I do that, He becomes my Strength and my Helper. I let Him take over and work through me, flow through me, and create through me. He is never stressed - think about that! Some of my best work has happened by just leaning into Him. That way, we burn the oil of the Holy Spirit, which is the best fuel there is!

## Boundaries and Limits

There is a lot that has been written on setting boundaries and limits. We do need to know our limits and recognise the signs of stress. Prolonged heavy stress is not good. Short bursts can be coped with, but when it is never-ending, you start pulling against it. Know when to relax, catch up, and have a day away. We need to know our limits and set some boundaries (some margin) for our own wellbeing. Holidays and breaks need to be regularly planned into your work life, as part of your work, not an extra when you have time. Know what is therapeutic for you – and make sure you schedule regular therapeutic times that will recharge your emotional tank. (There is more about this under "Prosperous Soul.")

It is vital to know your OWN limits, not someone else's – and these will grow as you stretch out and grow in confidence and in God. You will find yourself able to handle more and more. I've been amazed as I've allowed God to stretch me and expand my capacity to cope. I have been through massive times of stress and stretching, and I have been amazed at how God has expanded my capacity to cope because I have let Him. So, know your limits, but also allow God to stretch you that bit more each time. Slowly does it is the key – don't push it until all of a sudden you crash in a big heap (which I was really good at). Learn the warning signs and know when it is time to slow down.

Boundaries are another area we can give over to the Holy Spirit. I have needed to let Him take me further and help me push those boundaries. I wouldn't have done many of the things I have been able to in my life and wouldn't have increased my capacity like I have if I hadn't been led by the Holy Spirit. From someone who had lived a very restrictive, fearful life, who didn't handle stress at all well and had a very small capacity, I can and have accomplished huge challenges and major stretching with my Personal Coach by my side, cheering me on. It is important that we are burning the oil of the Holy Spirit. When we run on empty and attempt to do too much in our own strength, that's when we burn the oil of the flesh.

We can be the freest and most exciting people in the world because we have such a trustworthy and faithful Father. Let's not get so locked into the familiar that we have no expectation of anything different. The faith life is one of adventure, expansion, trust and surprise!

## THE ROAD OF LIFE

***(picture you and Jesus on a mountain bike)***

*At first, I saw God as my observer, my judge*
*Keeping track of the things I did wrong,*
*So as to know whether I merited heaven or hell when I die.*
*He was out there, sort of like a president.*
*I recognised His picture when I saw it,*
*But I really didn't know Him.*
*But later on, when I met Christ,*
*it seemed as though life were rather like a bike ride,*
*but it was a tandem bike,*
*and I noticed that Christ was in the back helping me pedal.*
*I don't know just when it was that He suggested we change places,*
*but life has not been the same since.*
*When I had control, I knew the way,*
*It was rather boring, but predictable…*
*It was the shortest distance between two points.*
*But when He took the lead….*
*He knew delightful long cuts, up mountains,*
*And through rocky places, at breakneck speeds.*
*It was all I could do to hang on!*
*Even though it looked like madness, He said, "Pedal!*
*I worried and was anxious and asked,*
*"Where are you taking me?"*
*He laughed and didn't answer,*
*and I started to learn to trust.*
*I forgot my boring life and entered into the adventure*
*And when I'd say, "I'm scared,"*
*He'd lean back and touch my hand.*

*He took me to people with gifts that I needed,*
*Gifts of healing, acceptance and joy.*
*They gave me gifts to take on my journey,*
*My Lord's and mine.*
*And we're off again.*
*He said, "Give the gifts away; they're extra baggage, too much weight."*
*So I did, to the people we met,*
*and I found that in giving, I received,*
*and still our burden was light.*
*I did not trust Him, at first,*
*in control of my life.*
*I thought He'd wreck it;*
*but He knows bike secrets,*
*knows how to make it bend to take sharp corners,*
*knows how to make it jump to clear high rocks*
*knows how to fly to shorten scary passages.*
*And I'm learning to shut up and pedal in the strangest places,*
*and I'm beginning to enjoy the view*
*and the cool breeze on my face*
*with my delightful constant companion, Jesus Christ.*
*And when I'm sure I just can't do any more,*
*He just smiles and says… "Pedal!"*
Author unknown

It's time to take the brakes off and let Jesus take control! Like Ronan Keating sings: "Life is a rollercoaster, you've just got to ride it!" How do you ride a rollercoaster? You sit back, relax and take the brakes off.

# KEY 18

# "HOLY SPIRIT - MY PERSONAL COUNSELLOR"

JOHN 14:15-16 CALLS Him the "Paraclete" which means "Comforter, Counsellor, Guide, Teacher, Helper, Encourager, Advocate, Called Alongside One."

Who can help us overcome our seemingly endless list of problems? Who can help us find the love we need when we feel like we just don't have any more to give? Who can help us get inside our own skin to deal with low self-esteem, multiplied memories of failures and mistakes, inadequacy, childhood fears relived, the need for love and approval, rejections, performance standards, self-punishments, guilts, self-judgments, restless disapproval of ourselves and our shortcomings, daily decisions about the expenditure of our time, energy and money with long-range implications?

Who can share the load, the burden with us and has enough wisdom for all the crossroads and decisions we have to make in our life?

Where can we turn to receive comfort and counsel in our times of trial? Who can we trust? Can we trust anyone to understand our deepest fears and insecurities?

To whom do we go when we have an aching need for strength, courage and confidence? Someone who will listen and understand? Someone who will allow us to talk until we know what we're trying to say. Someone who will probe to the hub of the issue, who has the authority and wisdom to help us see any confusion in our thinking or distortions in our emotions. Someone who leads us to the truth about ourselves and our lives and empowers us to act on that truth. Someone who has the power to heal our painful memories, sharpen our vision of what's best for our future and catch us up in a purpose beyond ourselves - one that's big enough to fire our imaginations and give ultimate meaning and lasting joy to our daily lives.

That's a tall order!

No friend, psychiatrist, psychologist, pastor, parent or spiritual advisor can meet all these qualifications. But there is ONE who has all these gifts. He ALONE has the omniscience, omnipresence and omnipotence to be the kind of counsellor we need.

He is the Holy Spirit! The Greatest Counsellor in the whole world! He's always available. He loves you no matter what. He never has a bad day or hasn't got time for you. He never makes a mistake. He can help you change. He can help you with your problems, relationships and decisions, for He knows everything. He is always with us, for He never sleeps. He has all power to give us strength and courage. He is the Holy Spirit with us and living within us. The Greatest Counsellor in the World.

*"And I will ask the Father, and He will give you another Counsellor to be with you forever - the Spirit of Truth... He lives within you and will be in you."*
(John 14:15-16)

A human counsellor learns listening skills, how to draw a person out, and how to communicate unqualified acceptance. That's exactly what the Holy Spirit does for us in an infinitely deeper way when we give Him a chance by BEING COMPLETELY HONEST WITH HIM - allowing Him to lead us to deeper truth about ourselves and our thoughts and feelings.

He is the MOST AMAZING PERSON. He is the All-Knowing One - He gets it right every time. He doesn't have to spend hours trying out different theories.

He doesn't have an answerphone or put you on hold.

I have 24 hours a day, seven days a week, unlimited access - no peak or off-peak charges - no internet clog - no running out of data - no traffic jams - straight through **every** time - He's my **lifeline!!**

He is gracious. He doesn't intrude. He is patient. And yet, He is SO POWERFUL! He is the "rushing wind," the "breath of life".

Stop trying to live your Christian life in your own strength and walk with your Counsellor. The Holy Spirit is not the power of God; He is God. He is a Person like Jesus is a Person.

The more we realize that the Holy Spirit is a Person, the more we will treat Him as a Person, and the more we do that, the more He will respond to us as a Person. This new relationship is crucial. While Jesus was on earth, His disciples went to Him freely for help. Now we are commanded to boldly approach the Father in Jesus Name. This direct access to the Father is accomplished only through the Person of the Holy Spirit.

This has been and still is the greatest secret and strength of my life - getting to know the Holy Spirit as my Personal Encourager and my Personal Counsellor, and so much more. He is my constant companion and my closest, most intimate friend.

With everything within me, I want to encourage you to get to know the Holy Spirit. Build your relationship and intimacy with Him and let him be the Best Counsellor in the World to you.

At any time of the day or night, draw near to Him, and He will draw near to you. Pull Him in, lean in close, and He will wrap Himself around you (that's the only way I can describe). Being consciously aware of Him 24/7, even to the point where, at times, no words are needed. He gets us - we just know each other heart to heart.

If there was one thing I would want you to know, that I could pass on to you, it would be this - get to know the Holy Spirit as your Personal Encourager, Personal Counsellor, Personal Trainer, Teacher and Guide.

# KEY 19

## "YOUR PAST CAN BECOME A HITCHING POST OR A SIGNPOST"

You can live your whole life tied up to the hitching post of your past, never being able to get past that. With that victim mentality, you can blame everything and everyone else on why you are like you are.

But Jesus says you're free. You are set free by the blood of the Lamb. The chains are broken. You can even sing those words in church, but you refuse to unhitch yourself from the hitching post of what was done to you. You're tied up there, and you're not going anywhere.

OR, you can turn those things around and make them into a signpost that points other people to Jesus Christ. "Look how Jesus has set me free! I once was that... but now I am this!" Turn your mess into a message, and see God draw many other people to Himself.

There's an old story about two boys who had a father who was an alcoholic. They grew into young men, and one son became an alcoholic: "What choice do I have?" he said. "My father is an alcoholic."

The other son never touched a drop of alcohol. "How could I?" he said. "Look what it did to my father."

Two boys, same dad, two different perspectives. One made his upbringing his hitching post. The other made his upbringing a signpost.

Your perspective in life will determine your destination.

In the Old Testament, Moses expresses his anger and frustration because the Israelites were "hitched up," camped out and refusing to move. This trip to the Promised Land could have been completed in eleven days, not 40 years! The Israelites, it seems, had the same problem we often have trouble with today. They had decided to drive down stakes, hitching their "horses" of past practises and general unbelief to the hitching posts of the past.

The Lord spoke to Moses: *"How long will this people provoke me? And how long will it be before they believe me, for all the signs which I have showed among them?" (Numbers 14:11)* God had enough and spoke to Moses: *"You stayed long enough at this mountain."* In other words, move on! Yes, it was horrendous and had the power to ruin your life, but only if you let it. You can make it work for you. Stop going around and around the same old post, the same old issue, the same old disadvantage syndrome, the same old offense, the same old ways of thinking, when Jesus has broken those chains. Turn that hitching post into a signpost.

We want to be ones who live life with a freshness every day, forgetting the past, leaving behind the "dead horses" tied to the old hitching posts. I could still be in that place, tied to all those old "hitching posts" of childhood abuse, fear, blame, living as a victim, depression and oh so many insecurities. But instead, I have allowed Him to take them and turn them into a signpost for others to find freedom in Him.

He turned my absolute mess into a message, and He can for you too. He can **"Turn your Scars into Stars".**

# KEY 20
## "ATTITUDE OF GRATITUDE"

> *"Gratitude is the ability to experience life as a gift. It opens us up to wonder, delight and humility. It makes our hearts generous. It liberates us from the prison of self-preoccupation. Gratitude is not something we give to God because He wants to make sure we know how much trouble He went to over us. Gratitude is the gift God gives us that enables us to be blessed by all His other gifts, the way our taste buds enable us to enjoy the gift of food. Without gratitude our lives degenerate into envy, dissatisfaction, and complaints, taking what we have for granted and always wanting more." (John Ortberg)*

Science has proven that people who express their gratitude daily are 25% happier and significantly healthier than those who don't. Gratitude is a huge depression-buster. Like that old hymn, "Count your blessings, name them one by one...and you will be surprised at what the Lord has done."

The Psalmist said in Psalm 77:11: *"I recall the many miracles God has done for me. They are constantly in my thoughts. I cannot stop thinking about them."* Notice, he said thoughts of God's goodness were constantly in his mind. That's a great way to live!

Too often, though, we remember what we should forget - our disappointments, hurts and failures - we dwell on all the negative things about a person, about our family, about our upbringing, about our finances, about a church, about our workplace or our occupation, about our marriage, our relationships - and we forget what we should remember - our victories, successes and the good times.

In the Old Testament, God commanded His people to celebrate certain feasts so they wouldn't forget what He had done for them, and so they could pass on those inspiring stories to the next generation. Several times a year, the Israelites stopped whatever they were doing, and everybody celebrated how God brought them out of slavery, or how God defeated this enemy, or how He protected them against that calamity. These celebrations were not optional - they were commanded, and the people were required to attend and remember God's goodness to them.

It would do you good to review God's goodness to you on a regular basis - simply thinking about the major victories in your life, the unexpected successes, or the times when you knew that God intervened in your circumstances.

Remember the day your children were born.

Remember how God gave you that job.

Remember when God brought that special person into your life.

Remind yourself how you fell in love and got married.

Thank God for your spouse and your family.

Remember what God has done for you.

Remember the moments where God has touched your life.

Remember your church. Sometimes people are so ungrateful and so critical of their church. It's God's Plan A. He doesn't have a Plan B. He loves His church!
Remember the times someone has encouraged you, prayed for you and helped you on your way when you were down.
Remember those who have discipled you and cared about you - helping you through your struggles. Remember their love and unconditional embracing and acceptance of you.
Remember those who watch out for you, teach you, follow you up when you're lagging a bit.
Remember those who challenge you when you're getting off track.

Remember those encouraging pats on the back that helped you on your way.

Remember those who faithfully serve you week after week, year in, year out.

Remember the number of times you have walked in the doors of church and your spirit has been lifted.

Remember the worship times that have lifted you and the precious times in the Holy Spirit.

Remember the messages that have helped shape your life and the revelation you have received from the Word of God, the faith moments when something life changing has dropped into your spirit, the special God moments.

Think about how much you have grown.

> Think about the fun, social times - laughing, doing life together, holidaying together, having fun, the fellowship times, the special bonding times, the special people God has brought into your life, the moments you've enjoyed together (the laughter and the tears).
> Remember the life moments along the way, the weddings you've got to enjoy, the 21sts, the engagements, the baby showers, the bridal showers, the loving gifts that have been showered on you for birthdays, and the milestones in people's lives.
> Remember the projects you've worked on with others. The special times of prayer together, sharing your hearts and dreams.
> Remember the many ways your leaders have gone out of their way for you, perhaps going out of their way to pick you up or to phone you. The ways people may have blessed you with food, meals, gifts, cards, prayer, hugs, even money at times.

You need to do this often and on purpose. There are too many people standing at the Complaints Counter and way too few standing at the Thankfulness Counter. When we learn to recall the good things God has done, it helps us to stay in an attitude of faith and to remain grateful. It's hard to go around complaining when you are constantly thinking about how good God has been to you. It's hard to get negative and to veer off into unbelief or self-pity when you are always talking about God's blessings and favour in your life.

I encourage you to keep a notebook and when something happens in your life that you know is God, write it down. If God opened a door for you - add that to your list. Times you know He spared your life or spoke to you a specific word of direction - make a note of that, too. When you were down and discouraged, ready to give up, and God quickened a Scripture to your heart, and it lifted your spirits. Write that down. Keep a running record of the good things that God has done for you.

It needn't always be something big - to others, it may seem quite insignificant, but you know it is God guiding your life. Then on a regular basis, get that notebook out and read about all the great things God has done in your life. You will be encouraged! Otherwise, we are too good at forgetting what we should be remembering and remembering what we should forget.

Especially in times of difficulty, when you are tempted to get discouraged, get that notebook out and read it again. If you do that, you will not go through the day discouraged and defeated and your faith will rise. You will know that God is in control of your life. He is holding you in the palm of His hand, and He will take care of you.

The Bible reminds us, "*For it is God who is all the while at work in you.*" *(Phil. 1:6)*

Many times, God is working, and we may not recognise it. This helps us to become more aware of God's goodness. When you get a good break, when things change in your favour, when you find yourself at the right place at the right time, recognize that this is not mere coincidence but God directing your steps. If you'll be aware, it will encourage you and build your faith.

Every one of us can look back in our lives and see critical moments that had to be the hand of God. God arranged for me to be in the band playing the piano at a particular event that Ian was at, and then a week or so later, He had me go to a particular dance at the Mangapiko Hall (where I had never been before) - just five minutes down the road from where this amazing farmer lived. God also arranged for this farmer to be enticed along to this dance that same night.

I think about years before - as kids, we both played sports at the annual Combined Primary Schools Sports Day at Ngahinapouri - and God was looking on and thinking - see that girl over there - and that guy over there - they don't even know each other yet - but one day they're going to be married and serving Me together. (And we weren't even born again then!)

When you are tempted to lapse into negative thoughts and attitudes, turn it around and say, "I know God is working in my life. I know my due season is on its way and one day, I'm going to see all that God has been doing behind the scenes on my behalf." Then go out each day expecting good things, knowing that the Creator of the Universe is directing your steps.

*"Being confident of this, that he who began a good work in you will carry it on to completion until the day of Christ Jesus."*
*(Phil. 1:6)*

Believe that God is at work in your life, and then be on the lookout to see His hand shaping the events.

Even in our dark times, God is still working in our lives. Even when we don't think we'll ever smile again, God is there. He is the friend who sticks closer than a brother. He said He will never leave you or forsake you! (Deut 41:6).

You don't have to figure everything out. You may not know what your future holds - but you know who holds your future. God has been working behind the scenes in your life over the years and you can trust that He will continue working in your life now and in the years to come!

Whatever your circumstances are today, remember God's faithfulness and the way He has orchestrated good things in the past - He is working behind the scenes to arrange future events in your favour.

Learn to trust Him. Reject anything that hints at frustration or impatience. Remember, that when you believe, you activate His power. And keep in mind that just because you don't see anything happening, that doesn't mean God is not working. Remember the good!

Why don't you relinquish control and say, "God, I'm going to trust you. I know You have a great plan for my life." When you do that, you will feel an enormous weight lift off you. And you'll not only enjoy your life more, but you will see more of God's blessings and favour.

*"Gratitude unlocks the fullness of life. It turns what we have into enough, and more. It turns denial into acceptance, chaos to order, confusion to clarity. It can turn a meal into a feast, a house into a home, a stranger into a friend. Gratitude makes sense of our past, brings peace for today, and creates a vision for tomorrow."*
*(Melody Beattie)*

Thankfulness revives us and attracts the blessing of God! Gratitude is the secret to living a full life, and ingratitude is at the core of all sin. Gratitude produces joy.

Studies have shown that being thankful improves our physical and emotional health, boosts our immune system and increases blood supply to our heart. The daily exercise of keeping a gratitude journal can increase our alertness, enthusiasm, energy and improve our sleep. People who describe themselves as feeling grateful tend to suffer less stress and depression than the rest of the population.

*"I will give thanks to you with all my heart, O Lord my God.*
*I will honour you forever because your mercy toward me is great."*
*(Psalm 86:12-13 GW)*

# KEY 21
## "MAKING GOD BIG"

*"Oh, magnify the Lord with me, and let us exalt His name together!"*
*(Psalm 34:3)*

Often, we are standing at the wrong end of the telescope, making all our problems seem so huge, and God seem so small. We have shrunk Him down to the size of our problems, or even smaller. We have shrunk our theology down to the level of our circumstances, rather than lifted our circumstances up to the level of our theology.

It is time to turn the telescope around and focus on the bigness of God.

God is already BIG… IMMENSE… INFINITE… ETERNAL... LIMITLESS! We can't make Him any bigger than He already is, but we can enlarge Him in our own eyes, in our own perspective, and in our own thinking.

Making God BIG (as He already is) is so powerful. It blows the roof off your thinking, your mindsets, and the atmosphere over your head. And what's more, it puts God back where He rightfully belongs! In the light of His greatness, our problems and difficulties that seem so overwhelming can become petty, trifling, minute, trivial, paltry, insignificant, and microscopic.

He is bigger than our problems. He is bigger than any opposition. He is bigger than any disease. He is bigger than any questions we have. He is bigger than our frustration. He is bigger than our struggle. He is bigger than our crisis.

It does not take much to magnify God. Just read His Word. Read it out loud. Read it until it begins to take hold in your heart. Read it until it is personal. Read it until it reverberates in your spirit and dominates your mind. Read the Psalms. Read the Proverbs. Read of the battles He has won. Read of His mighty acts and His valiant deeds. Read of those who believed Him and how they overcame. Meditate on the power of our God.

- When God is made BIG, problems are made smaller.
- When God is made BIG, demons tremble, cower and flee.
- When God is made BIG, diseases shrivel.
- When God is made BIG, mountains are moved into the sea.
- When God is made BIG, darkness is dispelled by light.
- When God is made BIG, answers to questions come easily.
- When God is made BIG, confusion lifts and direction comes.
- When God is made BIG, idols topple.
- When God is made BIG, unbelief gives way to great faith.
- When God is made BIG, the weakest Christian becomes mighty.
- When God is made BIG, there are no enemies that can intimidate and no devils than can operate.
- When God is made BIG, the frailest among us becomes a mighty overcomer.

He is the same God yesterday, today and forever. He hasn't changed. He has always been good. He is still good. He is still gracious, loving and kind. He is still merciful and abounding in goodness. He still does miracles. The God who did miracles in the Old Testament and was manifest through Jesus Christ in the New Testament (and performed great signs and wonders) will do them for us.

- Our God is mighty.
- With God, nothing is impossible!
- What is impossible with men is possible with God.
- It is impossible for God to lie.
- It is impossible for Him to deny His own nature.

- It is impossible for Him to fail to do what He promised He would do.
- There is no difficulty He cannot overcome.
- There is no stronghold He cannot bring down.
- There is no bondage He cannot break.
- There is no prison He cannot open.
- There is no need He cannot meet.
- There is no mountain He cannot move.
- There is nothing too hard for our God!

When we make God BIG…

- We become a much bigger person.
- We're more secure, steadfast, unmoveable, unshakable, resolute.
- We worry less, and we're more settled in our spirit.
- We're more forgiving, more attractive, more inspiring.
- We have a bigger heart for people.
- We're more relaxed, trusting, joyful and adventurous.
- We enlarge our vision, our worldview, and our capacity.
- We become more open, and we extend more grace.
- We have greater peace, resilience, energy and passion.
- We have greater faith, authority, power and anointing.

How big are you? How big is your God? How big is your God in you?[11]

(Excerpts from Wendell Smith's book, Great Faith)

*"Those who know their God shall do exploits."*
*(Daniel 11:32)*

11 Note: If you would like a free printable to pray through and familiarise yourself with the bigness of God, please feel free to email me or download from my website.

# KEY 22
# LEARN SOME RELAXATION TECHNIQUES

JESUS CAME TO teach people about abundant life. To possess this quality of life, one must have peace of mind and something that is even deeper than that - peace of soul. Inner serenity, mind and soul quietness can counteract the ill effects of this troubled world.

## Don't Take Tomorrow to Bed with You

Matthew 6:34 teaches us to take one day at a time, to not concern yourself about any presumed evil thing that may happen, for if that feared day comes; it will either care for itself, you will know how to deal with it, or God will handle it. It doesn't mean we shouldn't plan ahead, for that would be unrealistic, but definitely not in the couple of hours before bedtime, and certainly don't take the issue to bed with you and let it disturb your night's sleep, for nothing can be done about it tonight anyway. Be careful how you spend your hour before bedtime, by deliberately preventing your mind from being agitated by problems. Spend the last hour before sleep in light and pleasant conversation with your loved ones. Watch carefree tv or read a carefree story, then spend fifteen minutes with the greatest of all books - the Bible. Some find it helpful to read a Psalm every night.

It may help to repeat this affirmation: "I now cease mental consideration of any problem." You can then visualise all matters as being put aside. Go to sleep in the conscious thought and affirmation that whatever you may be called upon to handle the next day, God and you can and will do together. Relax in God's protecting care. In faith and trust, let God give you rest.

1 Peter 5: 7 says to *"Cast all your anxiety (some versions say burdens) on Him because He cares for you."* Make sure you pray before going to sleep and hand everything over into His capable, strong hands. He will be working on it while you sleep peacefully.

I remember hearing international evangelist Luis Palau share how every night before going to sleep, he forgives anyone who has done him wrong that day, asks forgiveness for anything he has done wrong, and casts all his burdens on the Lord. He then sleeps like a baby all night long. This is a good practice to get into, and one that will bring the *"peace that surpasses understanding." (Phil 4:7)*

## Relaxation Techniques

To properly rest, it is necessary to know how to relax muscle tensions. One suggestion that worked for me is a relaxation technique developed by the famous psychiatrist, Dr Smiley Blanton. Whenever I found myself starting to get stressed or tied up tight like a rubber band, waking up worrying in the middle of the night, it was helpful to have something I could do to take my mind off my problems, and instantly bring relaxation. I would find a place to lie or sit and do the following:

1. As you lie on your bed, spend a moment or two clenching your hands and opening them to rest limply. To relax a member of your body, it is first necessary to exercise it. The hands and forearms are centres of tension.
2. Work down your body, next with your arms, raising them or tensing them, then allowing them to fall limply as though you had no muscular control over them. The limper you can make them, the more truly relaxed they are becoming.
3. Stretch your toes, then stretch or lift your legs, then allow them to fall back limply. Do this several times.
4. Work your way down your body, including the head and neck

area and abdominal muscles, tensing or stretching each limb or muscle and then relaxing it to go limp.

5. Lean back and breathe deeply in and out several times. A deep breath tends to contract the diaphragm, and when quickly expelled, assists in relieving tension.
6. Upon completing these exercises, lie quietly, allowing your mind to touch upon every member of your body, at the same time thinking of each part as becoming more and more relaxed. This will induce deeper levels of relaxation.
7. Finally, think of some very restful scene. For example, hills shrouded in a misty haze, a peaceful lake gently lapping on the sandy shore, yourself floating on top of a still, calm pool of water. Picture yourself lying back in the strong and safe, everlasting arms of your Heavenly Father (He will hold you, He will not let you fall, you can let go), curled up on your Heavenly Father's lap, or gazing on the loving and eternal face of Jesus.

These relaxation exercises can be practised at intervals during the day, wherever you can find a quiet place, or before going to bed at night or during the night. I found you can even do it inconspicuously without other people around you realising, even if you have children playing around you. Sometimes I would lie back on the kids' slide or trampoline outside in the sun and relax under the fresh air and warmth of the sunshine while the children played.

Hundreds of people have found this method of relaxation effective in producing a state of quietness and rest. Practise regularly, so you have an instant go-to whenever you start to feel tense. You can practise this as many times as you need to.

It is said that the worst thing you can do when you're drowning is to kick and splash. The best thing you can do is to FLOAT. And that is what I have found so helpful in the Holy Spirit. Instead of kicking and screaming when you are anxious or stressed, just lean back into those "everlasting arms" the Bible speaks about, and float. He will catch you every time!

## Tranquillise Your Thoughts

At the close of the day's work, practise the feeling of tranquillity. It takes practise to put your mind into a tranquil condition, especially while you are still in recovery, but it will be achieved with persistent effort.

The first step is to deliberately conceive of the mind as entirely quiet. Think of it as the surface of a pond on which there is not the faintest suggestion of a ripple. Picture the mind as motionless and filled with deep quietness. Think in silence until an atmosphere of silence seems to surround you. Picture serene places; a lonely sea beach, a remote country road, a mountain lake.

I like to give my mind to the Holy Spirit, letting Him think through me. He is the Spirit of Peace, after all. I call it "gliding in the Spirit." When I didn't know what to think and my mind was all over the place, and I didn't want to think negatively or anxiously, but that was all my mind was wanting to do, I learned to put my mind into neutral (like you would your car) and "glide in the Holy Spirit," thinking nothing. When He controls my mind, He keeps it on an even keel. He doesn't think fear thoughts! He doesn't think anxious thoughts! He doesn't think negatively! He brings only good things to your mind. (You will find more on this in the section on "Stinking Thinking".)

Practise actually "receiving" the gift of Christ's peace. Do that by repeating His words, personalised:

*"Peace I leave with (your name), My peace I give to (your name); not as the world gives, do I give to you, (your name).*
*Let not your heart be troubled, neither let it be afraid."*
*(John 14:27)*

When Jesus said, before He left this earth, "Go in peace." The correct translation of that is, "Go *into* Peace."

Another way to tranquilise your mind is to make a mental list of the numerous times God has been good to you. You can do it on paper as well if you like, but it is especially good to get you thinking on the list of God's good deeds. For example, recovery from an illness, the guidance that helped you take the right course of action, the time your loved one was divinely protected, the occasion when in deepest discouragement, you found a way out of difficulty. Affirm: "Since God has helped me so many times, I will continue to count upon His amazing kindness."

Another idea is to walk out the scripture: *"Surely goodness and mercy shall follow me, all the days of my life." (Psalm 23:6)* Picture goodness and mercy following you around.

Repeat these practices regularly (even daily), and you will be amazed by the new tranquillity of your mind.

# KEY 23

## "A CHECK-UP FROM THE NECK UP"

**This is a bigger bite than some of the others because it is SO HUGELY IMPORTANT! I really hope I can show you the importance of your thoughts. This was the biggest key for me, and the one that I had to work the hardest on to become well.**

*"As a man thinks in his heart, so is he."*
*(Prov. 23:7)*

You are what you think about! It's amazing that one little thought, one little reminder of something good - or bad - can trigger a whole chain of reaction through our nervous system and change our whole countenance.

Our emotions are so powerful. They can either rejuvenate us or drain us, and they influence whether or not we're going to approach life with an attitude of victory or an attitude of defeat, but it all starts with the thoughts in our minds. When we dwell on the **wrong things** - negative, self-defeating thoughts - it makes us **weak** and **uncertain** and **fearful** in our minds. Negative emotions get stirred up, and we waste precious time and energy. But when we dwell on the **right things**, when we believe God and meditate on His promises, we become **strong** in our minds. We uplift and encourage ourselves as the Bible commands. Our emotions stay balanced, and we are able to approach life with an attitude of faith and victory.

I encourage you today to take inventory of your thought life. I never realized how negative my thoughts were (and subsequently, the words out of my mouth) until I started taking inventory. When I started thinking about what I was thinking about, I realized it was no wonder I was sick, fearful and depressed all the time!

Each of us thinks thousands of thoughts every day, but they are not all positive or beneficial. I learned to become like a film censor and censor out the thoughts or parts of the film that were negative or not beneficial. Clip them out and instantly discard them. Don't give them a second thought! Let them go.

I had to be particularly vigilant about fearful thoughts, as one wrong thought would send me spiralling down into depression. That's how powerful thoughts are - they can send your whole system into an involuntary panic attack or high anxiety. That's what the Bible means to take every thought captive. Don't let every thought in your head have free reign. Censor them.

Pay attention to almost any conversation for about ten minutes, and you will hear toxic self-talk, whining, commiserating, self-pity, excuses, blaming, condemning and justifying. I have noticed a huge trend toward this, especially amongst our younger generation, even in the church, today. You can take control over your thoughts relatively easily, but consistency is the difficult part. It may take a while to master it, but you can! Keep at it, and you will be amazed at the results and how much better you feel.

Fill your mind with God's Word, and you will have no room for Satan's lies. Let the Word of God make your mind strong. Don't focus on how big your problems are; instead, focus on how big your God is! Get your thoughts and words going in the right direction so you can stand strong in your mind and move forward in the path of victory God has prepared for you. I have great news for you - you no longer have to be a slave to your thoughts!

*"...take captive every thought to make it obedient to Christ." (2 Cor. 10:5)*

Life coaches will tell you that all lasting change in our lives is preceded by changed thinking. Any other type of change will be only temporary. The place to begin, then, is with your thought life, with a revival of your mind.

We spend very little time thinking about what we are thinking about. For most of us, thinking is a poorly developed ability that often occurs with little conscious awareness. Most of the time, we pay very little attention to the quality of thoughts passing through our minds. Few people have worked on having intentional, focused thinking. Instead, we need to give ourselves a "check up from the neck up."

**Your mind is such a valuable thing.**
**You need to protect your mental health at all costs!**

Because most people are oblivious to their habitual way of thinking, they experience less joy and a less abundant life than God intended for them. How many of you know there are a lot of things in life you have no control over? There is one thing in life that you DO have complete control over - your thinking! This profoundly influences every other aspect of your life.

The Bible describes our minds using the picture of a ship looking for a harbour. Though you may be unable to keep disease-ridden ships from sailing back and forth on the ocean, you can refuse them docking privileges in the harbour of your mind.

- Job talks about those who harbour resentment in their hearts.
- The Psalmist talks about those who harbour malice in their minds.
- James talks about those who allow bitter envy and selfish ambition to harbour within them.
- Jeremiah 4:14 (NLT) says, *"How long will you harbour your evil thoughts."*
- Deuteronomy 15:9 says, *"Be careful not to harbour this wicked thought."*
- Matthew 9:4 says, *"Why do you entertain evil thoughts in your mind?"*
- Romans 13:14 says, *"Clothe yourselves with the Lord Jesus Christ,*

*and do not think about how to gratify the desires of the sinful nature."*

Your mind is the most valuable thing that you have in your possession. The way you spend your mind is of utmost importance. You will become what you think!!!

Marcus Aurelius said, "The most important things in life are the thoughts you choose to think."

I also have to tell you a very important fact. Your mind is under siege every single second of the day. There is a great plan to control your thinking. In the course of time, you will become on the outside what you believe on the inside. The devil loves to take advantage of a mind that is ignorant or one that is pushed around by wayward emotions. As J. Oswald Sanders says, "The mind of man is the battleground on which every moral and spiritual battle is fought."

Scripture has much to say about our mind:

*"…casting down imaginations, and every high thing that exalts itself against the knowledge of God, and bringing into captivity every thought to the obedience of Christ…"*
*(2 Cor. 10:5 KJV)*

*"Let this mind be in you, which was also in Christ Jesus."*
*(Phil. 2:5 KJV)*

*"Thou wilt keep him in perfect peace, whose mind is stayed on thee: because he trusts in thee."*
*(Isaiah 26:3 KJV)*

*"Jesus said unto him, Thou shalt love the Lord thy God with all thy heart, and with all thy soul, and with all thy mind."*
*(Matt. 22:37 KJV)*

Behind everything you do is a thought, and each individual thought contributes to your overall character. How well your mind works dictates how much joy you experience, how successful you feel, and even how well you interact with other people. No area of your life is untouched by your thoughts! Your thoughts can become totally different, and as a result, your character can change, and your life can be transformed. God wants you to be completely alive, full of passion and bursting with joy!

## The 4:8 Principle

In his excellent book, 'The 4:8 Principle: The Secret to a Joy-filled Life' Tommy Newberry teaches that God's way of life is about thinking differently to the world; thinking in a way that is in alignment with heaven, in a way that maximises your potential.

If anyone was justified in being negative and overwhelmed, certainly Paul was. Unfairly accused, confined in prison, and facing death, he chose to emphasise possibilities, instead of problems. In his letters, he challenged believers to think differently and rise above the world's standard (and often the majority of the church, I might add). He presents us with exceedingly wise advice for thinking like God thinks when he challenges us to seek out and dwell on the positives in our life. Philippians 4:8 reflects very crisply the nature and character of God, who himself is true, noble, just, pure, lovely and of good report:

*"Finally, brethren, whatever things are TRUE, whatever things are NOBLE, whatever things are JUST, whatever things are PURE, whatever things are LOVELY, whatever things are of GOOD REPORT, if there is any VIRTUE and if there is anything PRAISEWORTHY - meditate, think on these things."*
*(Philippians 4:8)*

As Christians, we are called to meditate on things that mirror God's character!

Not only does this keep us from focusing on sinful or harmful things, but it also allows us to fill our lives with hope and optimism.

This is the way you revitalise your minds! This is the way you get unstuck from disagreeable conditions. This is the way you leave your mark on your family, your marriage, and on your world!

Mental discipline is the ability to keep your thoughts consistently focused. When you use Philippians 4:8 (the 4:8 principle) as the filter for your thinking, you focus on God and goodness to the exclusion of all else. As a result, you will begin to develop mental strength.

With high levels of mental discipline, you'll reach your goals faster, upgrade your potential for joy, and become a lot more fun to be around.

## FIX your thoughts

*Fix your thoughts on Jesus"*
*(Heb. 3:1)*

We need to fix our thoughts on Jesus. I think of it like supergluing my mind on Him, instead of all the other thoughts that can race through my mind.

When you're looking at Jesus - you're looking at the answer. Some people spend all their time looking at the problem. Instead, when you keep your thoughts fixed on God, the things of God will naturally permeate your life, and your goals will be in line with his will and his kingdom.

Without the positive focus of your thinking, even relatively easy goals become a strain to reach. With weak mental muscles, the existence of joy in your life is random and unpredictable. Mental laziness destroys your potential.

There is no need to be perfect - all you have to do is concentrate on progress.

By deliberately working to improve your mental game, you will steadily upgrade every area of your life! With strong, toned mental muscles, you'll become more fit spiritually, emotionally, relationally and physically.

Almost everything that happens to you, good or bad, originates with a single thought. Research indicates that the average person thinks approximately 50,000 thoughts per day and neuroscientists can now demonstrate that every thought sends electrical and chemical signals through your brain, ultimately affecting each cell in your body.

Thoughts can influence your sleep, your digestion, your pulse, the chemical makeup of your blood, and all other bodily functions.

The secret conversations you hold in the privacy of your own mind are shaping your destiny, little by little. With every thought that races through your mind, you are continually reinventing yourself and your future. This is either good or bad news because every thought moves you either toward your God-given potential or away from it. No thoughts are neutral.

Whatever you direct your mind to think about will ultimately be revealed for everyone to see. Remind yourself with a smile that *"my thoughts are showing."* What you persistently think eventually and inevitably crystallises into the words you speak and then the things you do. Every thought you have shifts your life in a particular direction, sometimes in a minor way and sometimes in a major way.

Unfortunately, approximately 90 percent of the thoughts you have today are repeats from yesterday and the day before. This is the primary reason why effecting permanent, positive life improvement tends to be met with such stiff resistance in most people. Right thinking is a choice you have to make for yourself for the rest of your life! If you are committed, you can select your thoughts and thereby shape your life here on earth into something spectacular.

## Mind renewal

Repentance is to turn away from one pattern of thinking and turn to another. I may come alive in a moment, but I'm changed when I renew my thinking and mindset. It's time to take that mindset and align it with what God says about you.

Romans 12:2 tells us that transformation is the result of a renewed mind.

> *"Do not conform any longer to the pattern of this world, but* ***be transformed by the renewing of your mind.*** *Then you will be able to test and approve what God's will is - his good, pleasing and perfect will."*

Unfortunately, most people struggle to change or renew their circumstances (like losing weight, fixing their marriage, making more money), when they should be asking God to help them renew their minds. When our minds are renewed, circumstances take care of themselves.

The secret to living an exceptional life TOMORROW is purely a matter of thinking strong, joyful thoughts TODAY. The battle you wage against your human nature is an invisible one that will be won or lost in the mind.

I cannot overemphasise the importance of developing mental discipline - the battleground is in the mind. The devil is completely defeated and disarmed - the only weapons he has left are the fiery darts he fires at our mind - to send our thinking skewiff. Minute by minute, hour by hour, in the hidden workshop of your mind, you are constructing thoughts of good or evil, depression or joy, success or failure.

You are writing your own life story as a human being with each subtle and soundless thought you think.

Did you know you cannot be joy-filled without thinking thoughts of joy? You cannot worry without thinking worrisome thoughts. You cannot be afraid without thinking thoughts of fear. And from personal experience in my own life - you cannot be depressed if you don't think negative, depressed thoughts.

Can you remember a time when you were thinking of hope and happiness but felt depressed at the same time? Can you imagine acting lovingly while thinking bitter thoughts of anger and resentment? When you are thinking, you have only the present moment, the NOW. Think of it as the gift of the present!

The importance of right thinking is emphasised throughout the Old and New Testaments.:

*"...as a person thinks in his heart, so is he." (Proverbs 23:7)*

*"We must "keep our heart with all diligence, for out of it spring the issues of life." (Proverbs 4:23)*

*"We are warned that the things we intensely fear have a tendency to become reality. (Job 3:25)*

And Jesus repeatedly reminds us that what we receive will be the result of what we believe. In Matthew 15:18, Jesus taught that people are defiled or made unclean by what is in their hearts - in other words, by the way they think. Jesus knew well that persistently thoughts eventually lead to action.

So did Paul, who encourages us to *"take every thought captive to make it obedient to Christ." (2 Cor. 10:5)* Can you imagine a negative, cynical, self-defeating, or "woe is me", victim-mentality thought being obedient to Jesus Christ?

The illustration I like to give is to think of yourself accidentally dropping your hairbrush. You reach out and catch it before it reaches the ground. We need to be like that with our thoughts... take hold of them as soon as you feel them going south. Grab them and make them obedient.

Finally, James sums it all up when he writes that one who doubts is "*a double-minded man, unstable in all his ways." (James 1:8)*

If you desire to live a joy-filled life - a life that fulfils God's purpose for you - you must keep your thoughts fixed on the things of God. Can I suggest that the faith realm (the spiritual realm) is more "REAL" than anything in this earthly realm? If you want to get REAL, get into faith!

Yes, there is a time to be honest and share your deepest struggles with a trusted advisor or counsellor who will help you. But then get on and get into the faith realm!

*"The mind must be transformed from the earthly, natural and reasonable thinking that holds faith back – to heavenly thinking that releases us to kingdom living... Every thought and action in your life speaks of allegiance to God or to Satan. Both are empowered by your agreement. Renewing your mind means learning to recognize what comes from hell, and what comes from heaven, and agreeing with heaven. That is the only way you will complete your divine assignment. God designed your mind to be one of the most supernaturally powerful tools in the universe, but it needs to be sanctified and yielded to the Holy Spirit so you can carry out His designs, creative ideas, and plans in your everyday life."*
*(Bill Johnson)*

We always have a choice of what we focus on. There will always be some junk, and there will always be some greatness. There is good and bad in every life, every marriage, every family, every job, every church, every friendship or relationship, every task you put your hand to, every house you live in, every city or country you live in, every part of your life!

If you desire a future that is a lot better than your present, you will need to change a lot about the way you think....and **Say No to "STINKING THINKING!"**

# KEY 24
## "CHANGING CHANNELS"

EVERY ONE OF us has a mindset that we regularly and consistently lock into. Our background, our education, our culture, our home environment, and what we have fed into our minds has all gone into developing a personal mindset and behavioural pattern in our life. Some of us are very positive in our mindset, and some of us are very negative. Most of us have degrees of both.

The problem that most of us have is that we so often dwell in the negative area (thanks to the fallen nature of man). The Bible says:

*"I call Heaven and Earth to record this day against you, that I have set before you life and death, blessing and cursing, therefore CHOOSE LIFE, that both you and your children might live."*
*(Deut. 30:19)*

Most of us have this daily battle to choose between what is a blessing and what is a curse. What is going to bring forth spiritual life, and what is going to result in spiritual death?

I am grateful for the following helpful teaching snippets (intermingled with my own) I gleaned from Gerald Bradley in his book, "Changing Channels" (which is no longer in print).

When you turn on your television and observe something that is really evil and bad, what should you do? Now if you said, "turn it off!" that is the second-best answer. You see, when you turn it off, what is still running through your mind? The same picture most often. Therefore, the best answer is to CHANGE CHANNELS!

## Don't Just Clear it - Replace it.

This was a huge help to me. In my most difficult times, I would carry scriptures written on a piece of card, so I could pull them out and instantly change the channels in my mind from a negative one to a positive one. It helped to snap me out of the wrong line of thinking, and it flipped me onto the right channel.

It is called the "replacement principle". A person receives counselling and ministry, and comes into real release and blessing, but, and this is a big BUT - unless that person "replaces" what has been removed, he is actually opening himself up to an even greater problem!

A person's "house" (life) must be OCCUPIED so that when there is a cleanout, it must be REFILLED. So many individuals keep on going back to their pastor or counsellor, but never proceed further, and mostly end up in a worse state. They refuse, either through disobedience or ignorance, to realize they must "replace" and fill up, that cleansed area of their lives.

God is in the REPLACEMENT BUSINESS, and we must find God's replacement programme for our lives every time we have some "cleaning out ministry". Remember, don't just clear it – REPLACE IT!

## Put Off - Put On?

*"Put off the old man – (the unregenerate self) with its evil practices and put on the new man which is renewed in the knowledge and after the image of Him who created it."*
*(Colossians 3:9-10)*

Again, the principle of "replacement" is seen in this scripture. Decision and action are required. PUT OFF the problems, attitudes and characteristics of the old nature, and deliberately PUT ON the attitudes and characteristics of the new nature.

The Amplified version gives us another key truth and principle that we need to put into practice:

*"Clothe yourselves, with the new spiritual self which is ever in the process of being renewed and remoulded into (fuller and more perfect knowledge upon) knowledge, after the image and likeness of Him who created it."*
*(Colossians 3:9-10 AMP)*

This putting off and putting on program is a **continual process.** God's renewing and remoulding takes place every time we put on, and put in, God's truth and knowledge. It is knowing and applying truth, that sets us free (John 8:32).

## Conformed or Transformed?

*"Do not be conformed to this world - this age, fashioned after and adapted to its external superficial customs. But be transformed (changed) by the entire renewal of your mind – by its new ideals and its new attitude – so that you may prove for yourselves what is that good and acceptable and perfect will of God."*
*(Romans 12:2 ANT)*

This is truly one of the great challenges and secrets to the victorious Christian life. The JB Phillips translation says: *"Don't let the world squeeze you into its mould."*

We either get pressed into the "conforming mode" of the world, or we choose the "transforming mode" of God's program. This transforming mode is God's way for us to have an entire renewal of the mind and helps us to prove what is His good and acceptable and perfect will for our lives.

Friends, fellow students, business colleagues, family, along with the newspaper, radio, books and TV, and the internet – all can cause us to be conformed and moulded to the world's pattern of thinking and behaviour. This is why our priority input must be God's transforming program so that our pattern of thinking and behaviour are from God.

Daniel was trained and placed in a secular godless environment and could have easily been conformed to that world system, but his priority was his three times a day "transforming period" where he fellowshipped with and prayed to the Lord (Daniel 6:10).

## Territory Choice - God or Satan?

*"Neither give place, (ground or territory) to the devil."*
*(Ephesians 4:27)*

The moment we allow negative, angry or critical thoughts - indeed any thoughts that are not godly into our minds, we are giving ground and territory to Satan to move in.

Paul challenges us in Philippians 2:5 "*to have the mind of Christ.*" Again, we make the choice - Christ or Satan? The context of Ephesians 4:27 is specifically dealing with the attitude of anger and how that is a prime area for giving ground and territory to Satan. If we keep on that channel, we are really in trouble. Jesus illustrates this truth very clearly in Matthew 6:24 when He said:

*"No man can serve two masters; for either he will hate the one and love the other, or he will stand by and be devoted to the one and espies and be against the other."*
*(Matthew 6:24)*

You cannot serve God and man (that is deceitful riches, money, possessions, or what is trusted in). Jesus is specifically referring to the priority control area of your life. You can only give that priority "place" or territory to one person. Either to God, or to the devil, and his multiplicity of side-lining activities and attractions, such as deceitful riches. Jesus challenges us to choose who we will serve and to whom we shall give the first place in our lives.

## Christ or Self?

*"Put on the Lord Jesus and make no provision for the flesh to fulfil its lusts. Put a stop to thinking about the evil craving of your physical nature." (Romans 13:14)*

The two channels show up strongly once again in this scripture. When we lock into the "flesh," which is our human nature without God, we automatically allow this channel to flood our mind with ungodly and destructive programmes.

One of the definitions of the word "sow" is "to set in motion". Consequently, every time we lock into the "flesh" channel, we are setting wrong things in motion. The only answer is God's replacement programme – and that is "put on the Lord Jesus Christ!"

Practically, what that means is that we put on the thinking, the character, the attitudes and the behaviour of Christ. It means putting into practice what Jesus did in His life. Daily times of prayer and consultation with the Father, constant memorizing and applying the scriptures, fasting, seeking first the Kingdom of God in all decisions, and ministering to others in the grace and power of God. Make sure, each day, you put on the Lord Jesus Christ, and stay tuned into this channel.

## Rubbish or Rebuilding?

The leaders of Judah, along with Nehemiah, made a clear and accurate observation when they said: *"There is much rubbish and we are not able to work on the wall." (Nehemiah 4:10)* Nehemiah told the people:

> *"You see the bad situation we are in, and how Jerusalem lies waste and its gates are burned with fire. Come let us build up the wall*

*of Jerusalem....and they said let us rise up and build. So they strengthened their hands for the good work."*

Before they could rebuild, they had to clear the rubbish. Before you and I can change channels and rebuild, we have to clear the rubbish out of our lives. Let's face it - most of the programs we see on TV and the internet are rubbish. It has been analysed that the average TV soap program has an average of nine problems per programme. An accident, a life-threatening situation, a marriage break-up, someone committing adultery, murder, blackmail, lying, stealing, immorality, the list goes on. Some people feed on these soaps (or Mills & Boons romances) and wonder why they have such negative, depressing lives.

No wonder when they have a constant diet of mental rubbish! As somebody said, "I don't know why they call them soaps when they make you feel so unclean."

TV and internet-wise – you need to constantly change channels and get into some wholesome, uplifting, positive, Godly programmes, podcasts and videos, so you are building into your life and renewing your mind, God's way. So clear out the rubbish from your life and start rebuilding.

## Fear - or Love, Power and a Sound Mind?

Paul highlights one of the great changing channels principles in 2 Timothy 1:7 when he says to Timothy:

*"God has not given us a spirit of fear, but of power,*
*love and a sound disciplined, well balanced mind."*
*(2 Timothy 1:7)*

In everything we do in life, we either respond in faith or in fear. Fear was the first negative emotion that entered Adam:

*"God called unto Adam and said, "Where are you?"
Adam replied and said, "I heard your voice in the garden
and I was afraid, and I hid myself."
(Genesis 3:9-10)*

The effect of fear within us is one of the most destructive forces that we can set in motion. Emotionally-induced illness or psychosomatic diseases have their breeding ground in a spirit of fear, and as a believer, we must learn to constantly change channels from a spirit of fear to the channel of love, power and a sound mind.

Anxious thoughts and fears can come from many sources. An unhappy home situation, a violent parent or spouse, a physical assault, unemployment, a hospital situation, a health difficulty, a death, grief and loneliness can all trigger off a spirit of fear.

The Bible says, change channels! God has not given you that spirit of fear, but He has replaced it with His love, power and a sound and balanced mind! What a privilege! This is why we must memorise the word of God and switch on to God's promises and provision. Remember:

*"A man does not live by bread alone...but by every word
that proceeds out of the mouth of God."
(Matthew 4:4)*

## Wrong Imaginations - or a Christ Controlled Mind?

Paul, in 2 Corinthians 10:5, focuses on one of the most difficult areas of the Christian life – controlling your thoughts and imaginations. And who does not have a battle at various times in these areas? The Apostle directs us to change channels when he says:

*"Cast down imaginations (thought patterns) and every high thing that exalts itself against the knowledge of God, and bring into captivity (and control) every thought to the obedience of Christ." (2 Cor. 10:5)*

What a challenge! The dictionary defines "casting out or casting off" as "to eject, to expel, to evict, to throw out, to get rid of, to drive out, to root out, to empty out, to clean out." Paul says to *"Cast off the works of darkness." (Romans 13:12).* And Jesus says, *"It is the thought life that pollutes – and makes you unfit for God." (Mark 7:20-23 LB)* Wrong imaginations and thought patterns set in motion destructive attitudes. Our thoughts will either take us into triumph or into tragedy. Therefore, to change channels, we must agree with what God says in the Word.

On this truth, make the following daily decision "to agree with God and disagree with the thinking of the world, your carnal self, and the devil." When you start operating on this daily programme, you are really bringing your thoughts and your thought life into the control and obedience of the Lord Jesus Christ. Solomon sums it up in Proverbs 4:23 in the Good News translation, when he says:

*"Be careful how you think, your life is shaped by your thoughts." (Prov. 4:23)*

So, shape your future, by changing channels from wrong imaginations, to a Christ-controlled mind.

## Hearers or Doers?

Jesus challenges us to be *"Doers of the word, and not hearers only, therefore deceiving our own selves." (James 1:22)* One of the great tragedies in the Christian church today is that we have many hearers, but very few doers. This verse tells us that if we only hear the word, and don't act on it and apply it in our lives, we are living in deception.

If our beliefs do not affect our behaviour, they are unbiblical. If your knowledge does not become applied knowledge, it is not biblical. If you are a hearer only and not a doer, you are living in deception. Remember, the Bible was given, not for information, but for transformation. Today, we have multitudes of informed believers, but very few transformed. God's programme for us is summed up in Romans 8:29, when Paul declares that we should be "...conformed to the image of the Lord Jesus Christ." (Romans 8:29)

Because you and I are not naturally conformed to the image of the Lord Jesus Christ, this requires a change, and to achieve this, we must change channels from being hearers only, to being doers and obedient to the word of God. As the Moffat translation of James 1:22 says, *"Act on the word!" (James 1:22 Moffat)*

## Carnal and Fleshly - or Spirit Controlled?

> *"The mind governed by the flesh is death, but the mind governed by the Spirit is life and peace. The mind governed by the flesh is hostile to God; it does not submit to God's law, nor can it do so. Those who are in the realm of the flesh cannot please God."*
> *(Romans 7:5-11)*

If we try to live the Christian life in human effort, we will fail miserably. We will experience condemnation, hopelessness, entrapment, burn out and exhaustion. The "flesh" mindset is dominated by I, ME, and MINE. It is selfish in outlook. Everything is centred on self and how we can satisfy ourselves. Its dominating influences are set against God. A mind set on the flesh will produce carnal behaviour. A mind under the control of the Holy Spirit, however, will produce the fruit of the Spirit - *"love, joy, peace, patience, kindness, goodness, faithfulness, gentleness and self-control." (Galatians 5:22)*

## Remain Locked Into God's Channel

On the short-wave radio bands, it is very easy to pick up several radio stations within a very short distance on your dial, and you often have to keep adjusting your channel, to stay on the desired station. Today, spiritually, there are so many voices out in the world, and it is so important to stay tuned in, and locked in, to God's channel. Isaiah declares that…

*"God will guard and keep us in perfect peace,*
*if we have our minds stayed on Him."*
*(Isaiah 6:3)*

The word "stayed" in the original means "stake". They would tie an ox or similar animal to a stake, and it would be safe, but if it broke away from the stake, it could cause all sorts of damage. If your mind is locked and anchored to the stake, which is God, you will be safe, and receive His wonderful peace. But if your mind breaks away from that stake (God and His Word), you will be in real trouble. So, make sure you remain tuned and locked into God's channel!

To practically illustrate how to change channels, I want to give you twelve areas that you can work on and make a deliberate choice to switch over to and onto God's channel. (Email me or visit my website for a free printable.)

# KEY 25
## PRACTICE HIS PRESENCE

*"One thing have I asked of the Lord, that will I seek, inquire for, and insistently require: that I may dwell in the house of the presence all the days of my life; to behold and gaze beauty, the sweet attractiveness and delightful loveliness of Lord and to meditate, consider, and inquire in His temple."*
*(Psalm 27:4)*

This verse is one of my absolute favourites! My constant go-to. I love God's Presence so much that I have learned to consistently and consciously withdraw into it and be enveloped in it, no matter where I am or who I am with.

No one has ever improved upon the method of Brother Lawrence, saintly character of the Middle Ages. He was a humble man, a cook, who found peace even in what may seem a menial and monotonous activity in the monastery where he lived and served. I have loved reading about him and what he lived. The method he taught is to simply to believe that always, at any hour of the day or night, in whatever circumstance of condition, Jesus Christ is actually present. At first, this may seem a beautiful fantasy, but as the idea is practised, it becomes an amazing and glorious reality. Not only great saints like Brother Lawrence, but everyday people have found it to be true. The Presence IS with them!

When you retire for the day, pull up a chair alongside your bed and imaginatively believe that Jesus Christ sits there beside you. This is not far-fetched, for He said, *"I am with you always." (Matthew 28:20)* Talk with Him just as you would if some loved one were sitting in that chair or on the edge of your bed. Ask Him all your questions, tell Him what is on your heart, then imagine what His answer would be if He spoke with the tongue of flesh. Soon you will have no doubt that He does speak with you, and you will sense and feel His presence with certainty.

The poet, Wordsworth, had the habit of imagining how it would be to talk to Jesus. What would be the look on His face, the tone of His voice? So real did Jesus become to him as a result of this practice that he actually felt the Master was His close companion and friend.

At intervals during the day, and especially at night, practise His presence, and it will become real to you also.

This is something that has helped me so many times over the years. I have had the most amazing and indescribable times with the Lord, where He has profoundly impacted my life. There is something about speaking to Him face to face, like He is right there on that chair next to you, rather than a "nebulous" God up there in the sky somewhere. Your prayers change, your tone of voice changes, the words you use change. It's like you are speaking to your dearest friend and caring about His heart as well. The tender interaction with your Lord and Master changes everything!

When you especially feel the need of the presence of Christ, read His words from your Bible. It might be best to use a New Testament in which His actual words are in red. This will enable you to quickly read His words in sequence. I have often done this, and it gives an amazing feeling that He is with you - actually talking to you. The feeling of comfort will be so profound, the actuality of His presence so tangible that you will feel deeply relaxed and at peace.

Should you be awakened in the night, assume the Lord wants to say something to you, knowing that you are more receptive when relaxed. Simply lie quietly, letting Him speak to you. And when He has given you His message, you can return to sleep.

Some of my "best ideas" have come during those times. That is not surprising because ideas get through most effectively when a mind is rested. The practice of His Presence produces creative quietness in addition to profound inner restfulness.

"A place of tranquillity is a place of creativity."

Cultivate a daily practice of spending time with Jesus. By encountering His presence, I have overcome debilitating fear and anxiety, suicidal thoughts and low self-worth, plus so much more. I learned how to hear God's voice and discovered His heart to comfort, lead, shepherd and empower His children. I learned about meditating on Scripture and how declaring the Word can transform the mind and enable us to better manage stress. With that newfound courage and sense of identity, He taught me to take bigger risks, step out in faith, and trust Him to show up in powerful ways. My regular prayer is, "Lord, if Your presence doesn't go with me, then I don't want to go, BUT as long as you are with me, then everything will be ok."

I remember praying that prayer constantly when heading to the other side of the world to speak at a Women's Conference in London. The presence of God was so strong in my daily prayer closet that I was so aware I didn't want to go to the other side of the world and not have that with me all the way. And of course, on the other side of the world, He was with me just as powerfully because He has already promised, "I will never leave you nor forsake you."

Whether you call it a quiet time, a daily devotion, or something else, this practice of pressing deeper into the presence of God will transform your life.

# KEY 26

## "INCH BY INCH, EVERYTHING'S A CINCH; YARD BY YARD, IT'S WAY TOO HARD."

THERE ARE MANY times in life when everything seems so overwhelming. The journey or task ahead seems just way too huge and daunting. During these times, I learnt to practise just focusing on one moment, one day, one step, one task, one part of the process at a time. And then the next step, and then the next step. Utterly refusing to think about the daunting big picture looming so large in front of me, I just kept focused on the small stepping-stone.

That is how I got through my days in the early stages of feeling so defeated and not knowing if I could fight my way out of that place - not knowing if I could even get through tomorrow.

That is how I got through my fourth pregnancy - one month, one week, one day, one half-hour, sometimes even one moment at a time. I can do that! I can do this next moment! And doing that next moment then gives you the courage to do the next, and so on.

Just break it down like the old saying, "How do you eat an elephant? One bite at a time." That is, after all, how marathon runners or ultra-marathoners tackle their huge challenges. Otherwise, because of your awareness of your weakness, your low capacity or your lack of confidence, and because you are too hard on yourself, you can just give up and think, "I can't do that! It's too huge. It's just too overwhelming to think about. I'd never be able to do that!"

As previously mentioned, I had to discipline myself to put Matthew 6:34 into practice. Taking one day at a time and refusing to think about tomorrow was a real discipline. Sometimes, I had to get down to taking one moment at a time, one half-hour or even five minutes at a time and refusing to think about the next half-hour or any further ahead. Just living in the moment, God and I could handle whatever was in that moment. This was a huge key for me that I still regularly use.

# KEY 27

## "BIRDS CAN FLY OVER YOUR HEAD BUT YOU DON'T NEED TO LET THEM BUILD A NEST IN YOUR HAIR"

THERE ARE THOUSANDS of thoughts that go through your head every day. Some experts estimate that the mind thinks between 60,000-80,000 thoughts a day (who counted?) The thing is, you don't have to give ALL of them a "second thought." Just let the negative ones keep on flying over. Only let the positive ones stay and let the rest keep on passing through. Don't beat yourself up because negative thoughts come - that's almost impossible to stop - just don't give them the time of day. Don't let them hang around and start to fester or build a nest in your hair. Just let them fly on past.

The more you fill your mind with positive things like the Word of God, uplifting and encouraging news and uplifting and encouraging music, for example, the less negative thoughts you will have.

### Get Rid of Stinking Thinking!

Think about what you are feeding your mind. Some people fill their minds with thriller movies, games with killing, constant bad news, depressing music or lyrics, hanging out with toxic or negative people, listening to gossip and people's stresses and dramas, or depressing social media posts. They then wonder why they have trouble controlling their mind. If you put the garbage in, then what will come out is garbage. "GIGO" = Garbage in, Garbage out.

Just as you (potentially) watch what you feed your physical body, watch carefully what you feed your mind with.

There was a point in my recovery when I decided not to watch the evening news. I just didn't want to fill my head with more depressing wars, murders, deaths, natural disasters, crashes, or the state of the economy when I was struggling to control my negative thoughts. The news just seemed like a constant repeat of a negative life and a depressing prognosis of the future out ahead, and I didn't need that. I just wasn't at a place to handle it then. The same would go for social media today. Recent studies have shown that people are much happier when they take a break from social media. But even on a "normal" day, you should still regulate what you regularly feed on or allow into your mind. You have the control. Just switch it off or change the channel. Remember… GIGO!

"None can destroy iron, but its own rust can.
Likewise, none can destroy a person, but his own mindset can."
(Ratan Tata)

Stay clean spiritually. Be aware of what you are exposing yourself to, like a watchman on guard over your eye and ear gates, spiritual atmospheres, your house, and your household. Use your spiritual authority - wield that sword of the Spirit, the Word of God. We have authority as we're **under** authority. I don't mean looking behind every bush for demons, but not being spiritual naïve/ignorant of the devil's schemes. Stay spiritually sharp and wide awake to spiritual atmospheres and deal to them straight away. They are like mice and will reproduce if you don't put a stop to them straight away. Give the enemy no landing ground - no advantage, no permission and no opportunity.

# KEY 28
## "GET RID OF YOUR DISADVANTAGE COMPLEX"

The following are excerpts from Robert Schuller's book, "Move Ahead with Possibility Thinking," that really helped me, intermingled with some of my own:

Get rid of ALL your disadvantage complexes:

**"I'm too old."** – The truth is, you are never too old to change. You are not too old to change until you give up. Only when you reach a point where you don't care anymore – then, and only then are you old. You are not old until you have lost your vision.

**"I don't have the time, money or energy to do what I'd like to do."** Are you sure? Or is that just locked-in thinking? Have you even tried? What if you disciplined yourself a little more and eliminated the wasted time, money and energy?

**"I am from a lowly background."** So what? No one's background or past is a disadvantage unless he makes it so in his thinking!

**"I came from a broken home. I had an awful childhood."** Let's face it – all of us come from dysfunctional backgrounds (when you look at it in the light of the Fall).

**"My skin's not the right colour."** "I can never really do what I want to do because of my race." Is that so? What do you want to do? What do you want to be? You can do, or be, almost anything you can dream or desire. Don't let others around you pull you into their mould. Start by being the very best at whatever you do, now. In God's kingdom, heaven is the limit! Don't put ceilings on God!

**"I don't have a good education."** So what? First prizes don't always go to the brightest and strongest man. Again and again, the man who wins is the man who is sure that he can. Attitude is more important than aptitude.

**"I am a female."** I grew up in an era where women were considered lesser (somehow) and weren't permitted to take leadership roles. Thankfully, that never bothered Jesus, and thankfully that has changed a lot these days.

Jesus was (and is) the greatest women's liberator of all time. In the world of the first century, men thought very little of women. They questioned women's value to society and denied them respect and privileges in politics, marriage, economics, education and religion. In contrast, Jesus was more concerned about women's rights and privileges than His own:

- Jewish women were never instructed openly, yet Jesus taught women publicly.
- A Jewish merchant would not count money back into the hand of a woman in case he touched her and contaminated himself, but Jesus touched women to heal them.
- On several occasions, Jesus revealed major truths to women first.
- The resurrection, upon which Christianity is based, was first revealed to a woman.
- A woman had been bleeding for 12 years and was ceremonially unclean, but Jesus understood her desperate cry for freedom when she reached out to touch the hem of his clothing.

Even though you may have given your life to Christ, and have been a beautiful Christian woman for years, are you really reaching out for all that God has for you as a woman of God?

It takes the power of God to release us from the negative, locked-in thinking of these beliefs. **It takes guts to leave the ruts!** Is it possible that you are in a negative-thinking rut? Determine not to sink into one or more of the disadvantage complexes listed above. Climb out of those ruts. Tackle some exciting and new possibilities today!

"Great people are just ordinary people
with an extraordinary amount of determination."

My husband and I raised our children to believe there were no such words as "I can't". **"Think you can or think you can't, either way, you will be right."** As a result, each of them, now in their adult years, have continued to press through barriers, obstacles and challenges to pursue all that God has for them and not settle for excuses. It does my heart good when I hear them teaching their children the same. Any disadvantage, rightly handled, can be turned into an advantage!

Don't allow other people's words to become your excuses which keep you locked into a box. Also be aware of your own words over your life that are keeping you bound. We think, "That's just the way I am. I can't do that – it's not me, and I don't intend to try!" I used to be like that – I know! Decide you want to break all those limitations around your life and go as far and as wide and as high as God can possibly take you in your life. Living a "No Limits" life in Him is exhilarating.

*"Michelangelo is credited with 44 statues created in his lifetime, but he only finished 14 of them. Now you may be familiar with the 14 he finished – David, the Pieta, and Moses, to mention a few. But the 30 he never finished are very interesting… a huge chunk of marble and out of it is sculptured an elbow or the beginning of a wrist. The rest of the human form is still locked up in the marble. Another chunk shows a leg, with the thigh, knee, calf, heel and foot clearly chiselled out of the hard stone, but the rest of the body is still locked within. And then another one shows the head and shoulders of a man, but the rest of the body is still frozen inside.*

*Of all the tragedies in life, the greatest tragedy is for a person to live and die and never be told what his possibilities are. And then I thought of the possibilities still locked within me, and my enthusiasm for God's releasing power grew. Jesus Christ reaches us so that He can redeem us and release our possibilities! You are an unfolding masterpiece in the hands of God – the master sculptor! (Robert Schuller)*

# KEY 29
## "LIFE CAN MAKE YOU BITTER OR BETTER"

IT'S YOUR CHOICE! You can choose to remain a victim and allow the bitterness of what you have experienced continue to eat away at you or limit you for the rest of your life, or you can choose to get better.

I, and no doubt you, have come across many a bitter and cynical person. For many of them, it has destroyed their health. Life has made them bitter and negative, and it shows all over them. You almost know what they are going to say before they even speak it.

Many people live with a victim mentality throughout their whole life. It is always everyone else's fault. Yes, it wasn't your fault. Yes, you didn't cause it, and you definitely didn't deserve it. But it is your responsibility, and within your control, how you deal with it. Not theirs. If you remain bitter and locked up, that just causes the enemy to win.

Bitterness eats away at you. The Bible teaches, *"Watch out that no poisonous root of bitterness grows up to trouble you, corrupting many." (Heb. 12:15 NLT)*

These "roots" or strongholds of the mind don't just sit there. They grow, they multiply, they sprout other destructive tentacles, and before long, they are infecting everything else in your life - your outlook, your relationships, your mental and spiritual health, and your success. Bitterness is just like "Couch" (pronounced 'Kooch'), one of New Zealand's most noxious and hard-to-get-rid-of weeds. It entangles everything! It is something every gardener detests. You have to get rid of it at the first little sight of it. Any tiny piece of root will sprout, grow, reproduce and eventually take over.

Bitterness can grow and multiply in individuals, marriages, families, churches, businesses, communities and people groups. If left unchecked, it will take over, suffocate and destroy.

Instead, you can decide to become better! You choose to become a better person after what you've been through. You can't change it! You can't turn back the clock. It happened. But rather than becoming bitter and twisted over it, you can choose to become better through what you have been through. You can choose to come out the other side a much better, well-rounded, perhaps not-so-gullible, not-so-naive, wiser, more empowered, more well-adjusted person (you can add your own words here).

I honestly never thought I would say this, but the things I have been through have made me a stronger, more confident person with unshakeable faith and convictions. I am much more compassionate, much more aware of other peoples' needs and feelings, much less self-centred and more outward focused. Because of all the tearing down throughout my life, I was determined to have a "building up" family and culture. All of our churches have been "building up" churches. The Lord has expanded my capacity and enlarged my perspective, purpose and outlook on life.

Be careful to check if you have any bitter roots and be sure to pluck them out while they remain small. Sometimes, you are not even aware until you ask the Holy Spirit to shine the searchlight of His torch in there to root them out.

You too can choose to "become bitter or better." As you become better, you learn how to handle situations better. It is so much more energising and empowering to become BETTER!

Both my husband and I teach regularly on increasing the anointing. Just as it is the "crushing and bruising" that brings the oil out of the olive, so it is with the oil of the anointing. The attitude with which you go through the crushing and bruising of life and circumstances determines the level or increase of oil/anointing you come out with on the other side. This is a powerful key in making challenging circumstances work for you.

If you had to go through that thing, then make it WORK FOR YOU! Let it make you an amazing person! Make the devil pay! He will wish he had never touched your life because whatever he throws at you, you just end up becoming BETTER and more powerful.

Make it your life's project to become the best you than you can be!

# KEY 30
## "NEGATIVITY IS LIKE CANCER"

*"The thief comes to* ***steal, kill and destroy****, but I have come that you may have life abundantly, til it overflows."*
*(John 10:10)*

*"Out of the overflow (abundance) of the heart, the mouth speaks."*
*(Luke 6:45)*

*"Above all else,* ***guard your heart****, for out of it flow the issues of life."*
*(or "it is the* ***wellspring*** *of life.") (Proverbs 4:23)*

EVERYONE GETS TIRED. There are so many pressures and demands in life that we all go through it to differing degrees. But when negativity sets in, it is like a dangerous killer disease – it is carcinogenic; it spreads if it's not checked and dealt with in its very earliest stages. We can start thinking things like:

- "I can't go another step."
- "I can't keep up this pace."
- "I feel trapped."
- "Poor me."
- "No one else cares."
- "No one is doing as much as me."

It's so easy to get caught up in negativity and self-pity. Yes, there are incredible pressures in ministry, or at home with small children, in the workplace and indeed, everywhere. We can't always get off the wheel. But we must learn to stay positive and glide through in the Holy Spirit until we can take a break.

Fact - I have found that I **cannot** get depressed or discouraged if I don't think negatively! If I stop the negativity, nip it in the bud immediately, I don't go downwards. I know a lot of people don't want to hear that because negative thinking is what causes it! As I shared in my testimony previously, I was a very negative person, and it sucked me down the plughole constantly. Even if you are in that dark hole, it is always negativity that keeps you there. Even IF imbalance has taken place, even IF you've been that way a long time, if you give yourself the right positive environment, you CAN fight your way out. You CAN turn it around! It will be a fight, but I promise you, if you start censoring those thoughts and refusing negativity, you will eventually give your system a chance to heal.

Yes, you can get run down and exhausted and not take good care of yourself. But, even then, if you take positive steps to check your life and balance it, change your routine, add spice, regulate yourself, you also need to STAY POSITIVE. Whatever you do, don't sink into the negative because it is a downward spiral.

Tim La Haye, in his book, "How to Win Over Depression" says: *"A negative or harmful thinking pattern, if indulged over a period of time, can actually trigger the production of harmful hormones from the pituitary gland and can cause damaging physical illness that can make the depression worse."*

Negativity drains you quicker than anything else. Being a faith person energises you. There is no power of the Holy Spirit in negativity - you negate your prayers by the very negative words you speak.

Refuse to get negative. Censor your thoughts. I know it works! If you tell yourself you can't do it, you can't! I have been through so much stress, pressure and challenge, but because I refused to get negative, I was able to cope. And not just cope but thrive.

Burnout, depression, cynicism, deception, offense, backsliding, loss of vision are all symptoms of negativity. I have seen so many good people taken out over it, great marriages destroyed, really good churches and ministries destroyed.

People tell me all the time the problems with their marriage and all the faults of their spouses. For some, it is like a broken record. If you were to ask me about my husband's faults, I am sure they are there, but I would have to really think about them. I truly just don't focus on them. I'm sure he's not perfect, but I just don't dwell on them. He has far too many good qualities to focus on and celebrate. The same goes for my children. When you focus on the good, you draw out the good. You mine for the gold! And where things aren't so good, that's where faith comes in. You call out the good in them by re-wording things differently. You speak it over them and into them by faith until they become that. It's about believing in them. You see them as God sees them and draw that out. You become a goldminer.

People are the same with a new church, new house, new location, new job, or new friends. At the beginning, it's all wonderful, and they rave about it. But it is not long before all they can see is the negative again, all the faults, just like the last one. And before long, they hate that one too. They've destroyed it (in their thinking) with their negativity.

Some people will see the negative in everything, no matter how good it is. And, of course, there will always be the negative, IF you want to look for it. Somehow, they think they are "cleverer" than everyone else, that they have spotted the faults. Hello! There are negatives everywhere IF you want to look for them.

No matter how amazing something is, negative people will always find the negative. It excuses their own defeat.

**"Some people are like photographers,<br>always in the darkroom developing their negatives."**

I want to challenge you to listen for it:

- I'm tired.
- I've got no energy.
- I've got no money.
- I've got no spare time.
- I've got no clothes.
- I've got no friends.
- I've got no help.
- No one cares about me.
- No one contacted me.

Some people walk into the room, and they only see all the negative things. Who's not there, instead of who is! What you don't have, instead of what you do! It runs in whole families at times.

Don't allow your children to grow up with a negative bent because it will affect their mental health in the years to come. Life is tough, but we have got to raise positive children to cope with this negative world we live in. Otherwise, you are doing them great harm.

We made a decision years ago that we would create a positive-speaking home environment. We get tired, we slip up, we get grumpy at times, we find fault with each other - but because we are all so trained, it sticks out, and we get ourselves back on track. I don't think we could have coped with stuff otherwise. We taught our kids to re-word things in a more positive way. For example, we never said, "We can't afford it," like you hear a lot of people repeating day in and day out. Instead, we would say something like, "Let's pray and see what God will do," or "Not right this moment, but let's believe God." Otherwise, you are just locking yourself up into poverty, speaking negatively all the time about your finances. Instead of saying we couldn't do something, we taught them to "ask the creative HOW" question. "HOW" is far more creative than "can't". When you ask the creative "How" you can often find a way.

I tell you, from experience, negativity will take you down the plughole quicker than anything else! Conversely, you will live a much happier life if you look for the things to be grateful for and the positive things in any given situation, even the most negative situation. I know which way I would rather live my life!

- Negativity always reflects inner defeat.
- Negativity always justifies its own existence.
- Negativity always chooses your friends for you.
- Negativity always magnifies problems and distorts the truth.
- Negativity makes sweeping statements and unfair judgments.
- Negativity negates the Holy Spirit's work.
- Negativity pollutes its environment.
- Negativity sabotages your future and limits your present.

The devil always wants to "dis" you!

- Disappointment
- Disbelief
- Distress
- Disobedience
- Discontent
- Distrust
- Disharmony
- Disunity
- Discord
- Despair
- Destruction
- Distortion

I love what Joyce Meyer taught me: *"Decide to disappoint the devil by not getting disappointed."* It has worked for me in so many circumstances.

Matthew 12 says a bad tree produces bad fruit; a good tree produces good fruit. The negative person produces negative fruit. The defeated person produces defeated fruit. We cannot go further than where our soul is at. We will not rise above the level of our confession.

I have seen far too many people taken out or sabotage the really good things in their life because they have become so negative. You need to see it like cancer and nip it in the bud as soon as you hear it starting to make inroads in your life and speech. Recognise it in your life and don't let it hang around.

# KEY 31
## "YOUR PAST IS NOT YOUR FUTURE"

*"But one thing I do: Forgetting what is behind and straining toward what is ahead, I press on toward the goal to win the prize for which God has called me heavenward in Christ Jesus."*
*(Phil. 3:13-14 NIV)*

Too often, we are straining for what is behind and forgetting what is ahead. When we stretch back and try to make sense of all that happened in the past, we are bound to be frustrated. Constantly replaying, reviewing and rewinding, we build different scenarios of what might have been. It's like trying to walk forward while looking backwards.

We think, "If only I had done this or that... things would have been different." Yes, it is true, things may have been different, but you didn't do it differently and thinking about it NOW can't change it THEN. Your past, no matter how tragic or terrible, is gone. You can never reach back into it and change it.

Even the wonderful parts of your past are gone. Don't try to live in them and allow them to drain your life in the present. It will only waste your time and energy.

*"You can't go back and change the beginning,*
*but you can start where you are and change the ending."*
*(CS Lewis)*

God never goes back, though He is the only One who can. He goes forward. He is always looking ahead and moving beyond the present. When Adam fell, God didn't sit down and think, "Where did I go wrong?" I should never have planted that tree! I should have set up an angel to guard it. Now I am going to have to start over. I'd better figure this out, so it won't happen again." He explained to Adam and Eve the immediate and far-reaching consequences of their actions, yet even in the midst of this sad separation, He prophesied their redemption from the fall and the curse of sin (Gen. 3:15).

This is a tragic truth: You can spend your whole life figuring out why you messed up (or why someone else messed up), and still be messed up once you've figured it out. Unfortunately, knowing why doesn't necessarily mean we will ever make sense of what happened. Even if you discover the **why**, it still doesn't produce the power to change. You must know the **who**. You must move from the problem to the answer - Jesus!

In Isaiah 52:1-2, Israel had been taken into captivity for forgetting God, had committed all types of idolatry, had broken every kind of commandment, and were proud and haughty (14:1). They felt hopeless and forlorn, they were afraid God would leave them in their bondage, their guilt weighed so heavily on them that they doubted God could ever forgive their iniquity. Their failures were ever before them.

But when God spoke to them during their captivity, He comforted them and painted a very different picture - one of hope. He wanted them to stir themselves to believe He would once again restore them. He told them to **forget their past failures and unfaithfulness** (read Isaiah 54:4). God didn't say, "I want you to remember your shame and learn from it." He said, ***"Forget about it because I have!"*** He addressed their fears and said, "Don't be afraid. I won't let you be shamed, disgrace or humiliated. I won't remind you of your past, so don't let anyone else. Forget about it!"

In essence, God was saying - "You once were that, but now I have made you new, and soon you'll be this!"

You may have grown up in a family (or church, even) who never let you forget your failures and mistakes. Human beings conveniently and painfully have a good memory...when it suits them. God enjoys turning our wastelands into fertile plains, He has a plan for irrigating our arid land. (Isaiah 43:19)

When we set our hearts to pursue God and all that He has provided, all hell trembles. It is then that the enemy releases his onslaught of discouragement. **Constantly trying to turn us back**, he points to our past failures and fears. Discouraged, we often mistake the enemy's resistance as God's refusal to help us. God is not refusing. He is waiting on us. We need to decide today that we will no longer tolerate captivity and live in less than what Jesus' death provided.

Forgive yourself! Stop playing God in your life! Read Isaiah 52:1-2 and see the most striking point here. The woman's freedom utterly depended on **her** taking action, not God. God had already supplied everything she needed to attain her freedom, but she had to act on the message. It had to be mixed with faith. It's our choice - to believe or remain bound.

I found that all the time I kept talking about these things of the past, I couldn't seem to get past them. I had to leave them where they were, in the past. There came a point when I realized I had to change my confession and only dwell on the positive outcomes and perspective. If all these things had driven me into God and His truths, then they were working for me... and that was a good thing. They had shaped me to become a better person and a better mother.

I counsel so many people who are stuck in the past. I have concluded that sometimes people find it easier to live in the past than do the work it takes to move forward out of their current situation. God wants to move you forward. Are you writing your own unhappiness script by refusing to let Him hold your hand and do that?

True freedom comes by letting go of the past, closing the door on it completely and moving forward to your God-given destiny. The past cannot be changed, but the future can be whatever we want to make it.

**Declaration - "This day, I make a decision to fear and honour You, God, above all my past failures and over all that would seek to discourage or distract me."**

# KEY 32
## "IT TAKES GUTS TO LEAVE THE RUTS"

"Guts" = courage; pluck; determination; intestinal fortitude.

"Rut" = a furrow made by a wheel; a settled habit or way of living; a groove.

When we first took over our farm, the farm races needed a lot of work. In the mid-winter, they were absolute mud and slosh. The huge tractor wheels went deep down in the mud and had forced a very high ridge up the middle. When the drier weather came, the races would dry like that. We always had to drive in those ruts to get to where we were going. They were so deep and ingrained that we almost didn't have to steer the tractor. No matter which way you steered, the ruts would continually pull the tractor back into that path.

As a farmer's wife, I would regularly drive the tractor to help my husband over the farm. Once you got into the ruts, you had to stay in there. To turn left or right off the race and into a paddock was quite a mission. To leave the rut going straight ahead, you had to try and jump the wheels out of the rut by rocking back and forth and trying to leap the tractor up the side of the ruts. It was quite a task, and you had to be quite aggressive to succeed.

That's how I see the deep ruts that we have either purposely, or unconsciously, established in our lives. We've got to be quite aggressive and determined to jump ourselves out of them.

The other choice is to stay there and end up following the rut all the way to the end, finding yourself in a place where you didn't want to go.

A rut:

- something that is hard to get out of;
- the same boring track;
- the status quo;
- going with the flow;
- a religious habit of always doing something the same way;
- locked-in thinking;
- a low place or furrow you're trapped in;
- a grave with the ends knocked out.

For example:

- negative thinking
- disadvantage syndrome
- complacency
- apathy

- dull, boring, ordinary lifestyle
- mundane
- average
- mediocre
- so-so
- continual defeat and failure, "I can't"
- procrastination
- bad habit patterns (for example, smoking, alcohol, drugs, sexual sin, negative talk, low self-esteem, anger)

Ruts are sometimes comfortable, but they're not going to get you where you need to go. Sometimes we find it easier to live in the past than do the work it takes to move forward out of our current situations. But God wants to move us forward and out of our ruts. Are you writing your own unhappiness script by refusing to let Him hold your hand and do that?

As tough as they are to endure – valleys, ruts and personal trials help us to push through and change our lives. Christians should be the most daring adventurers! But we need to quit the excuses. One of the spiritual gifts is the gift of faith. God wants you to rise and take back your rightful inheritance, a people of faith and courage.

There will always be the naysayers, the negative people who say you can't do something, it can't be done, the bad report people. But who are you going to believe? Them or God? There will always be excuses, the reasons why not. But what I love is those who do it anyway, AGAINST ALL ODDS! What could you do for God, if you took the limits off? He is a 'no limits' God!!

*"**How long** will you wait before you begin to take possession of the land that the Lord, the God of your fathers, has already given you?"*
*(Joshua 18:3)*

It is time to "snap the traps." It is time to get out of the ruts. It is time to quit the excuses. It is time to kick down the boundaries around our lives. It is time to stop giving the devil lordship in your life. And to take back ALL that belongs to us in the Spirit.

*"The kingdom of heaven is forcefully advancing and forceful men (women) lay hold of it."*
*(Matthew 11:12)*

It is time to take God at His Word and allow Him to do what he does best – making something out of nothing!

**"If you always do what you've always done – you'll always get what you've always got!"**
**(David Riddell)**

My God can make something beautiful out of a mess, and He loves to transform peoples' lives – to do the impossible! I am strong in presenting my faith because I KNOW without a doubt that it works! Standing on the Word of God and the finished work of Christ WORKS! If only you would dare to believe.

Faith takes guts! Because you know just enough for the next step. What if I fail? Join the club. You have got to get comfortable being uncomfortable in faith because your flesh is always going to fight faith. Don't just talk about your problem - talk to it. Speak the promises of God to it. Speak the promise that goes with the problem. Say it until you believe it and say it until you see it! You've talked ABOUT it enough. Get a grit that says, "I'm going to get a Word, and I'm only going to speak that Word." And speak that promise until you see it.

It takes a lot of guts and a lot of God! I truly believe you can go from a place of fear and insecurities – to an exciting life of freedom, security, courage, faith and victory! It takes guts to leave the ruts, but you can do it in partnership with God.

# ACKNOWLEDGEMENTS

To MY GRAPHIC designer and daughter, Hannah Marchant, thank you so much for believing in me, for your contributions and being so excited to get this published. To my editor, Rachel Ross; my formatter, Glenn at Sarco Press; to best-selling authors Chandler Bolt and Lise Cartwright of Self Publishing School, plus all the online community who have been tireless in their encouragement, input and cheering me on – I couldn't have done this without you! To my enthusiastic launch team and all the faith-filled women in my life who have spurred me on to do this over the years. To the one who championed me the most, my husband and accountability partner Ian – thank you for valuing women like you do, for your confidence and investment in me, your constant support (and hugs) keeping me going through the hard bits. Thank you all for journeying with me in bringing a message of hope where it is so badly needed.

# RECOMMENDED READING AND RESOURCES


Meyer, Joyce. *The Battlefield of the Mind,* New York, United States: Little, Brown & Company, 2017.

LaHaye, Tim. *Spirit-Controlled Temperament.* Wheaton, IL, United States: Tyndale House Publishers, 1994.

LaHaye, Tim. *How to Win Over Depression.* Grand Rapids, United States: Zondervan, 1996

Treat, Casey. *Renewing the Mind 2.0.* Tulsa, Oklahoma, United States: Winters Publishing Group, 2017.

Treat, Casey. *How to Be Your Best When You Feel Your Worst. New York, New York:* Berkley Publishing, 2009.

Schuller, Robert. *Self-Love.* New York, United States, Berkley Publishing Group, 1969

Leaf, Dr Caroline. *Switch On Your Brain, The Key to Peak Happiness, Thinking & Health.* Grand Rapids, Michigan, United States, Baker Publishing Group, 2013.*

*Dr Caroline Leaf's Facebook page has regular posts of "Mental Self-Care Tips"

Newberry, Tommy. *The 4:8 Principle: The Secret to a Joy-filled Life.* Carol Stream, Illinois, United States. Tyndale House Publishers, 2007.

Bradley, Gerald H. *Changing Channels.* Auckland, NZ, G.H. Bradley,1991.

Murphy, Tori. *Narcissistic Mothers 101: A Beginner's Guide*, Kindle Edition, Amazon Digital Services, 2016.

Morrigan, Danu, *You're Not Crazy - It's Your Mother: Understanding and Healing for Daughters of Narcissistic Mothers.* London, UK: Darton Longman & Todd Ltd, 2012.

Morrigan, Danu. *Dear Daughter of a Narcissistic Mother.* London, UK: Darton Longman & Todd Ltd, 2017.

# FREE PRINTABLES AVAILABLE

email: **faithgirltransformed@gmail.com**
web: **https://faithgirltransformed.com/**

"Who I am in Christ"

"Faith Confessions"

"Changing Channels"

"Knowing God"

"Making God Big"

"Disadvantage Complexes"

# ABOUT THE AUTHOR

ANNETTE IS AN ordained pastor and has been in full-time ministry for 30 years alongside her husband Ian, during which time they have planted four churches, all of which have experienced significant growth through evangelism. She shares her husband's passion for building people, leaders and strong, healthy local churches which has included apostolic ministry throughout New Zealand and overseas. Her heart's desire is to see God's church rise to the magnificent House of God He intended; an influential, powerful, Spirit-filled, soul-winning and contagious church which represents Jesus well.

Annette carries a heart to see women released and rise to their fullest potential in God and has shared her life-changing message of faith and hope in numerous church settings and conferences. She loves to create beautiful environments for women to flourish and rise in who they are in God. One of her major strengths and passions is ministering and teaching on the Holy Spirit and Faith. A passionate teacher of the Word of God, she loves to see people built and trained in a solid doctrinal foundation. Over 30 years she has been a great trainer of leaders and has developed her own School of the Bible course which has been incredibly popular.

With a healthy marriage of 43 years, Ian and Annette regularly minister in the area of marriage and family and love to see couples enjoying all the fullness, fun and vibrancy God intended.

Another of her greatest delights is the hilarious and fun times they share together as a growing family. They have four married daughters and sons-in-law (along with nine delicious grandchildren) who share their vibrant passion for the local church and are all involved in various areas of fruitful church leadership. Caravanning at the beach, fun dates, long walks on the beach with her husband, reading, café-ing, movies and shopping trips with her girls, plus quality time with her grandbabies (and photo-booking them all), are her favourite ways to unwind and replenish.

Made in the USA
Monee, IL
15 March 2020

23218477R10138